Editor
Amethyst W. Gaidelis, M.A.

Editor in Chief
Ina Massler Levin, M.A.

Creative Director
Karen J. Goldfluss, M.S. Ed.

Cover Artist
Barb Lorseyedi

Art Coordinator
Renée Mc Elwee

Imaging
Ariyanna Simien

Publisher
Mary D. Smith, M.S. Ed.

GRADES 3-4

WEEKLY WRITING LESSONS

CORRELATED TO COMMON CORE STANDARDS

- teaches vital writing strategies
- organized by the week for easy use
- scaffolded to build writing independence
- incorporates formative and summative assessments
- whole-group, partner, and independent activities

Authors

Sandra Cook, M.A. & Helen León, M.A.

Teacher Created Resources
6421 Industry Way
Westminster, CA 92683
www.teachercreated.com
ISBN: 978-1-4206-2578-3

©2013 Teacher Created Resources
Made in U.S.A.

Teacher Created Resources

Table of Contents

Introduction

Building a foundation for writing begins with strategies and creative ideas. *Weekly Writing Lessons* gives the young author ideas and strategies for writing stories with strong introductions, transitions, conclusions, elaboration, and literary devices. Each strategy is introduced and developed over a period of five days. The lessons build on one another, culminating in a series of five writing projects that incorporate all strategies learned.

The format begins with direct instruction on the first day that introduces the student to the strategy. The teacher continues to model the strategy with the class on the next day. On the third day, students work with partners to delve into the writing concepts using various skills and techniques in a fun way. The fourth day provides the student with an independent writing assignment that includes instructional guidance. The five-day lesson ends with a writing assignment that the student completes independently. This plan can be used as a Monday through Friday activity, or teachers can begin the plan on any day and continue for five days. Students who are proficient writers, as well as those who find it difficult to get started with a writing assignment, will benefit from this five-day plan.

Five-Day Lesson Planner

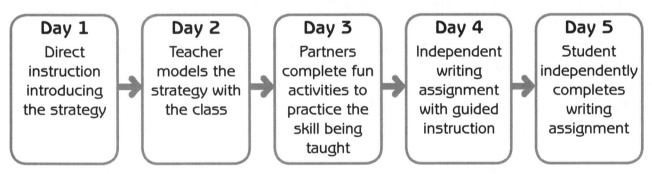

Day 1	Day 2	Day 3	Day 4	Day 5
Direct instruction introducing the strategy	Teacher models the strategy with the class	Partners complete fun activities to practice the skill being taught	Independent writing assignment with guided instruction	Student independently completes writing assignment

Additionally, *Weekly Writing Lessons* is a one-step resource for the teacher, providing complete five-day plans for developing writing strategies from the opening to the closing and in between. This comprehensive workbook eliminates the teacher's continual search for instructional writing materials. It was developed to meet the needs of both the teacher and the student.

Weekly Writing Lessons prepares students to communicate ideas in any writing format. The workbook is an essential resource to help students in grades three through four to meet the demands of today's standardized testing. More importantly, *Weekly Writing Lessons* teaches children valuable writing skills that will be used throughout their lives.

How to Use the Book

Weekly Writing Lessons is a writer's workbook for the young author, as well as a complete five-day planner for the busy teacher. The workbook consists of five chapters, each containing lessons on a particular concept of writing. Each lesson is taught over the course of five days of instruction. The workbook is comprehensive and easy to follow for both teacher and student. The chapters can be taught sequentially, or in the order that best meets the needs of the students.

Each lesson in *Weekly Writing Lessons* begins with teacher instruction. On **day one**, the teacher will introduce the lesson with a short explanation of what will be taught, an example of usage, and a list of vocabulary or phrases that will be used in the lesson. The teacher should preview the list with the class so the students understand the words or phrases that will be used in the lesson. The teacher will then guide the whole class in activities related to the strategy.

The teacher will model the writing skill on **day two**. A class paragraph will be created with the teacher. The instructor can display the paragraph during the teaching of the five-day lesson. The children can keep their copies in notebooks or binders to use as a reference for future stories.

Day three of each lesson is a partner activity. This activity can also be completed in small groups depending on the size and demands of the class. The activity uses the skill being taught in a fun and interesting way.

Independent writing will begin on **day four**. These lessons include guidance and a structured writing activity. This is an opportunity for the teacher to observe any problems or questions the class might have and make adjustments.

Day five has students using the writing skill to write a paragraph independently. They will be given story ideas and a list of vocabulary words or phrases that can be included in the paragraph.

Weekly Writing Lessons provides the students with strategies that can be used to write any story. It includes a format for planning what will be written, as well as ample opportunities for practice. The students will check their work at the end of the lesson and make revisions. There are many opportunities for the students to share what they have written with the teacher and class. The teacher will be able to use this sharing as formative assessment and adjust the instruction accordingly.

At the end of the book, there is a writing assessment. The students will use all the writing concepts taught to write five complete stories. A writing checklist is included to allow the student to check off the concepts that were used. Each story will take several days to complete, ending with a finished copy for the teacher to assess.

Each student's writing should be kept in a notebook or binder, or on a computer, if available. While space for writing is provided on individual worksheets wherever possible, students may need to write or finish activities on seperate paper. Throughout *Weekly Writing Lessons*, students are writing paragraphs that address a particular skill. These paragraphs can be used to inspire a complete story. In addition to these writing opportunities, a Story Ideas page is included at the end of the workbook to give the teacher and students numerous writing ideas.

Weekly Writing Lessons provides a resource for day-to-day writing lessons and equips young authors with skills and strategies to make them successful writers.

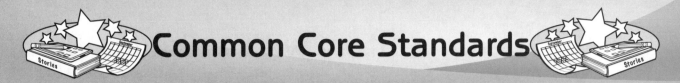

Common Core Standards

The activities in this book are correlated to the Common Core State Standards © Copyright 2010. National Governors Association Center for Best Practices and Council of Chief State School Officers. All rights reserved. For more information about the Common Core State Standards, go to http://www.corestandards.org/.

Grade 3 Writing	
Text Types and Purposes	
Standard 3: W.3.3	Write narratives to develop real or imagined experiences or events using effective technique, descriptive details, and clear event sequences.
W.3.3a	Establish a situation and introduce a narrator and/or characters; organize an event sequence that unfolds naturally.
W.3.3b	Use dialogue and descriptions of actions, thoughts, and feelings to develop experiences and events or show the response of characters to situations.
W.3.3c	Use temporal words and phrases to signal event order.
W.3.3d	Provide a sense of closure.
Production and Distribution of Writing	
Standard 5: W.3.5	With guidance and support from peers and adults, develop and strengthen writing as needed by planning, revising, and editing.
Range of Writing	
Standard 10: W.3.10	Write routinely over extended time frames and shorter time frames for a range of discipline-specific tasks, purposes, and audiences.
Grade 3 Language	
Vocabulary Acquisition and Use	
Standard 5: L.3.5	Demonstrate understanding of figurative language, word relationships and nuances in word meanings.

Grade 4 Writing	
Text Types and Purposes	
Standard 3: W.4.3	Write narratives to develop real or imagined experiences or events using effective technique, descriptive details, and clear event sequences.
W.4.3a	Orient the reader by establishing a situation and introducing a narrator and/or characters; organize an event sequence that unfolds naturally.
W.4.3b	Use dialogue and description to develop experiences and events or show the responses of characters to situations.
W.4.3c	Use a variety of transitional words and phrases to manage the sequence of events.
W.4.3d	Use concrete words and phrases and sensory details to convey experiences and events precisely.
W.4.3e	Provide a conclusion that follows from the narrated experiences or events.
Production and Distribution of Writing	
Standard 5: W.4.5	With guidance and support from peers and adults, develop and strengthen writing as needed by planning, revising, and editing.
Range of Writing	
Standard 10: W.4.10	Write routinely over extended time frames and shorter time frames for a range of discipline-specific tasks, purposes, and audiences.
Grade 4 Language	
Vocabulary Acquisition and Use	
Standard 5: L.4.5	Demonstrate understanding of figurative language, word relationships, and nuances in word meanings.

Begin a Story with a Sound Word

Bang! Crash! Splash! Ping! These are sound words. They imitate the sound that something makes. A writer often starts a story by using sounds to capture the reader's attention.

Example: *Knock, knock! Who could that be? Maybe it was Joe coming over to play. I ran to the door. When I opened it, I couldn't believe what I saw.*

Sound Words

roar	drip	buzz	meow	crack	smash	crunch	ring
boom	beep	squeak	snap	hiss	crash	creak	pop

Whole Group Fill in the blanks with the sound words from the box that make the best super starters for each story opener.

1. _____ ! Tiny animals scurried across the field.

2. _____ ! The bottle hit the floor.

3. _____ ! He was saved by the bell.

4. _____ ! A bee was flying around my head.

5. _____ ! I hit the ball, and the bat broke in half.

6. _____ ! The lion was chasing the zebra.

Independently When you use a sound word, it must make sense with the object. What sounds would these things make? Fill in the sounds. Use any sound words of your choice or find words from the list above.

1. car: _____   3. horse: _____

2. door: _____   4. ball: _____

Now it is your turn to write your own sound openers. Choose three of the sound words you just wrote down (above) and write an opening sentence for each one.

1. _____ ! _____

2. _____ ! _____

3. _____ ! _____

Whole Group Share your favorite sentence with the class.

Begin a Story with a Sound Word

Sound words imitate the sound that something makes. A writer often starts a story by using sounds to capture special sounds. These sound words will grab the reader's attention.

Whole Group Let's write an opening paragraph using "Beep!" as our **Super Starter Sound Word**.

Brainstorming Time!

A. As a class, make a list of things that make a "beep" sound.

1. _____   3. _____

2. _____   4. _____

B. Next, help think of an opening sentence for each of the topics in the above list.

1. Beep! _____

2. Beep! _____

3. Beep! _____

4. Beep! _____

Independently Decide which sentence to use as the topic for a paragraph. Which one do you think would make the best story? Why?

_____

Whole Group Vote for your favorite opening sentence.

The winning opening sentence is number _____ !

Now that we have the opening sentence, continue working together to complete the paragraph.

Beep! _____

_____

_____

_____

> ## Check Your Work
>
> Does the sound word make sense with the topic?
>
> Will the sound word catch the attention of the reader?

Begin a Story with a Sound Word

Sound words imitate the sound an object makes. Writers use sound words at the beginning of a story to grab the reader's attention.

Partners With a partner, circle all the sound words in the story below. Sound words are not always in the beginning of a sentence or paragraph.

Clip-clop! As I walked into the circus tent I saw horses prancing around the ring.

"Ladies and Gentlemen," the ringmaster was shouting, "Welcome to the greatest show on Earth!" Suddenly a small car came whizzing past me. Vroom! A clown was driving it and honking his big red nose. Another clown sat in a baby chair and broke it. Crash!

"Ha, ha!" I couldn't stop laughing. Growl! In the center ring, the lions roared loudly. Crack! The lion tamer's whip hit the ground, and the animals jumped back on their stands. Above all the acts, the trapeze was swooshing back and forth as the performers flew from one swing to the next. It was an amazing show.

Whole Group Share the words you circled.

Partners Now, with your partner, use sound words to complete the following poem. Use words from the paragraph above or make up your own.

The Circus

_____ ! The silly clown beeps.

_____ ! The ferocious tiger leaps.

_____ ! The excited audience cheers.

_____ ! The circus is here!

Independently A couplet is a poem with two lines of verse. Write a couplet about a fun place to visit using sound words of your choice or words from the paragraph above.

_____ ! _____

_____ ! _____

Check Your Work

Will the sound word catch the attention of the reader?

Whole Group Volunteer to share your couplet with the class.

Begin a Story with a Sound Word

A writer can use words at the beginning of a story that capture special sounds. These sound words will grab the reader's attention.

Independently Write an opening paragraph using the word "crash."

A. Use the opening sound word "crash" to write a sentence about each of the following objects.

1. dishes: _____

   _____

2. bicycle: _____

   _____

3. waves: _____

   _____

B. Select one of these sentences for your opening paragraph. Which opener would make the best story?

The opener that would make the best story is number _____ because

_____ .

C. Write an opening paragraph with the sound word "crash." It is important that the sound word makes sense with the topic you are writing about. Remember, you can use sound words throughout the paragraph.

Crash! _____

_____

_____

_____

_____

Check Your Work

Does the opening sound word catch the attention of the reader?

Did you use sound words anywhere else in the paragraph?

Whole Group Share your paragraph with the class.

Begin a Story with a Sound Word

Writers sometimes use sound words at the beginning of a story to grab the reader's attention. A sound word imitates the sound an object makes.

Sound Words

roar	drip	buzz	meow	crack	smash	crunch	ring
boom	beep	squeak	snap	hiss	crash	creak	pop

Independently Write an opening paragraph that begins with a sound word.

A. Choose a sound word to begin a story. Use any sound word of your choice or find a word from the list above. Don't choose a sound word that you have used before.

I chose the word _____ because _____

_____ .

B. Write down things, people, or animals that make the sound of the word you chose.

1. _____ 3. _____

2. _____ 4. _____

C. Write opening sentences for two of the topics in the above list.

1. _____ ! _____

2. _____ ! _____

D. Select the best opening sentence for your paragraph. Write an opening paragraph with your topic using the sound word you chose. Your sound must always make sense with the topic you are writing about.

_____ ! _____

_____

_____

_____

Check Your Work

Does the sound word make sense with the topic?

Does the sound word catch the attention of the reader?

Whole Group Share your paragraph with the class.

Begin a Story with a Question

What in the world was that? The answer could be, "That was a shooting star," or "I think that was a giant bee," or "That was a sonic boom." Beginning a story with a question is a great way to spark the reader's curiosity. The reader will want to continue to read to find out what will happen next.

Example: *"Where is my lucky shirt?" Andrew started throwing things all over. His room was never neat, but now it looked like a tornado had hit it. All of a sudden, he heard a knock on his door . . .*

Question Words

who	what	where	when	how	which	why	whose
did	do	is	are	were	could	would	was

Questions

Who should I take?   Where is it?   What is going on?

Are you kidding?   What time is it?   How did I get into this mess?

Whole Group We will start each of the following paragraphs with a question from the box. The question must make sense with the rest of the paragraph.

1. _____

This is the longest day ever. I just can't wait to go to the party tonight. Mom is supposed to drive me; unfortunately, she is not home.

2. _____

The movie is at 8 o'clock, and I can bring one friend. That should not be a problem, except that I have two best friends.

Independently Write a question sentence to begin each of these paragraphs. You may use the sentences above or come up with your own. The question must make sense with the rest of the paragraph. End the sentence with a question mark.

1. _____

Dogs are running down the street. Boys and girls are chasing after them, and I hear music.

2. _____

I know I did my homework, but it is not in my folder. If I get another missing assignment, I am in big trouble.

Whole Group Share your favorite question sentence with the class.

Begin a Story with a Question

Writers begin a story with a question to trigger the reader's interest and curiosity. The reader will continue to read to find out what will happen next.

Question Words

who	what	where	when	how	which	why	whose
did	do	is	are	can	could	would	should

Brainstorming Time!

Whole Group Let's read this paragraph and then complete it.

_____? *My friends are coming over in five minutes, and my little brother wants to play with us. I know I won't be able to get rid of him unless I do something fast.*

A. Think of two question sentences that could be used to fill in the blank.

    1. _____

    2. _____

B. Think about the opening questions. Which one would make the best opener for the paragraph? Vote for your favorite question.

    The winning opening question is number _____!

C. Next, let's make a list of events to include in the paragraph. The events should be written in the order they will appear in the paragraph.

    1. _____   3. _____

    2. _____   4. _____

D. Now it's time to complete the paragraph.

_____?

My friends are coming over in five minutes, and my little brother wants to play with us. I know I won't be able to get rid of him unless I do something fast. ____

_____

_____

_____

Check Your Work

Does the question have the reader wondering what will happen next?

Begin a Story with a Question

Beginning a story with a question is a great way to spark the reader's curiosity. The reader will want to find out what will happen next.

Partners   With a partner, practice identifying and writing questions.

A. Match the question with the answer. Write the letter of the matching answer on the line before each question.

1. _____ What are you doing?

2. _____ Can I go out and play?

3. _____ Where is my hat?

4. _____ How long did you wait for the bus?

5. _____ Which one did you buy?

a. I had to wait ten minutes.

b. I got the one with the stripes.

c. I am finishing my homework.

d. It is on the table.

e. You can go out after dinner.

The answers to these questions give you information. An interview is another way to get information. In an interview, a person asks questions to learn interesting facts and details.

B. Now pretend to interview a talking orange. Write three questions to ask the orange. Remember that good interview questions provide the reader with unique details about the character. The questions should not have a "yes" or "no" answer.

Examples

Bad: *Do you like hanging in a tree? Yes.*

Good: *What do you like about hanging in a tree? I like to swing in the wind.*

Question 1 _____

Answer 1 _____

Question 2 _____

Answer 2 _____

Question 3 _____

Answer 3 _____

C. On a separate piece of paper, write a paragaph using the answer information.

Check Your Work

Does the paragraph have interesting facts and details?

Whole Group Volunteer to share your paragraph with the class.

Begin a Story with a Question

Beginning a story with a question is a great way to spark the reader's curiosity. The reader will want to continue reading to find out what will happen next.

Question Words

who	what	where	when	how	which	why	whose
did	do	is	are	can	could	would	should

Independently Write a paragraph that begins with a question.

A. First, fill in the blank with a question word from the list above.

1. _____ you see that?

2. _____ is that noise?

3. _____ cleaned my room?

4. _____ is all my stuff?

B. Select one of the above openings to begin a paragraph. Which question opener would make the best story starter?

Number _____ is the best choice because _____.

C. Now make a list of events to include in the paragraph. The events should be written in the order they will happen in the paragraph.

1. _____

2. _____

3. _____

4. _____

D. Write an opening paragraph with the question opener you selected. Use the events you listed to complete the paragraph.

_____

_____

_____

_____

Check Your Work

Will the opening question spark the interest of the reader?

Whole Group Share your question opener with the class.

Begin a Story with a Question

A writer can begin a story with a question to trigger the reader's interest and curiosity. Starting with a question will have the reader wondering what will happen next.

Independently Write an opening paragraph using any question of your choice or find a question from the list below.

List of Questions

Where did I go wrong?	*Think — Did you get a bad grade or make a mistake?*
Did I win or lose?	*Think — Was it a race or a science fair project?*
What should I do?	*Think — How could you solve a problem?*
Why didn't I listen?	*Think — Did you get in trouble?*
Is this really happening?	*Think — Did you see something strange?*

A. Write the question you will use to begin your paragraph.

_____

B. Now make a list of events to include in the paragraph. The events should be written in the order they will happen in the paragraph.

1. _____   3. _____

2. _____   4. _____

C. Write an opening paragraph, beginning with the question and including the events above. Your question should have the reader wondering, "What's next?" Don't forget to use a question mark at the end of your sentence.

_____

_____

_____

_____

_____

Check Your Work

Will the opening question spark the interest of the reader?

Do your details support the opening question?

Whole Group Share your question opener with the class.

Begin a Story with Dialogue

"Using dialogue is a great way to start a story," stated the writer. Dialogue is the exact words that a character is thinking or saying. Dialogue can be funny, serious, or inspirational. Starting a story with dialogue will spark the interest of the reader.

Example: *"Smile," uttered the photographer.*

"No way! If I do, everyone will see my braces!" thought Karen.

Dialogue Words

whispered	screamed	exclaimed	announced	replied
laughed	screeched	yelled	explained	cried
answered	repeated	shouted	gasped	sighed

Whole Group What would a character say in each of the following situations? How would the character say it? Would he or she whisper, laugh, yell, or just reply? Using the words from the above list, we are going to write openers with dialogue.

Example: *Andrew broke his brother's toy.*

Andrew gasped, "My brother is going to be so mad."

1. Marie didn't know she had a test.

   _____

2. The lights went out and left you sitting in the dark.

   _____

3. Robert stepped on something squishy.

   _____

4. Tiffany saw her favorite movie star.

   _____

Independently Write Super Starter openers using dialogue for the following situations.

1. Pat was ready to go to the lake when it started to rain.

   _____

2. Richard sat on his lunch.

   _____

3. Sandy rode a horse for the first time.

   _____

Whole Group Share your favorite Super Starter opener with the class.

Begin a Story with Dialogue

Dialogue is the exact words that a character is thinking or saying. Writers can start stories with dialogue to spark the interest of the reader. Put quotation marks before and after the exact words of the character who is speaking.

Whole Group We will write an opening paragraph using dialogue. What would someone say in this situation?

The team won the championship game.

Dialogue Words

whispered	screamed	exclaimed	announced	replied
laughed	screeched	yelled	explained	cried
answered	repeated	shouted	gasped	sighed

Brainstorming Time!

A. Let's make a list of comments that the team players might say after winning the game.

1. _____   3. _____

2. _____   4. _____

B. Now we'll use two of the comments to write dialogue sentences. Add the character who is speaking and a word to describe how the comment is being said. Write the dialogue, putting quotation marks before and after the character's exact words.

1. _____

2. _____

C. Decide what dialogue to use in the paragraph. Vote for your favorite.

The winning opening dialogue is number _____!

D. Now, let's complete the paragraph.

_____

_____

_____

_____

Check Your Work

Does the dialogue help people understand the character?

Begin a Story with Dialogue

Dialogue is the exact words that a character is thinking or saying. Writers can start stories with dialogue to spark the interest of the reader.

Partners With your partner, write a paragraph that begins with dialogue.

A. First, unscramble each line of dialogue. Write capital letters and punctuation marks where they are needed in the sentences. Remember that quotation marks go before and after the exact words of the character who is speaking.

1. friend's may house Mary I go asked my to

   _____

2. got the Osvaldo play screamed I lead the in

   _____

3. girl the hurt cried knee I my

   _____

4. announced due is the your teacher Monday report on

   _____

B. Now select one of these dialogues for an opening paragraph. Circle that number.

C. Make a list of events to include in the paragraph. The events should be written in the order they will appear in the paragraph.

1. _____   3. _____

2. _____   4. _____

D. Use the dialogue you selected and the events from above to write an opening paragraph with your partner.

_____

_____

_____

_____

Check Your Work

Did you add details that support the opening dialogue?

Can you picture the character saying the dialogue?

Whole Group Share your dialogue with the class.

Begin a Story with Dialogue

Dialogue is the exact words that a character is thinking or saying. Dialogue can be funny, serious, or inspirational. Writers start stories with dialogue to spark the interest of the reader.

Dialogue Words

whispered   explained   screamed   sighed

Partners   Write opening dialogue.

A. Use the words above to practice writing opening dialogue. The words in the list describe how something is being expressed. Make sure the dialogue makes sense with these words. What would someone say in this situation?

The money for mom's gift is gone.

1. whispered: _____

2. explained: _____

3. screamed: _____

4. sighed: _____

B. Select one of these sentences for your opening paragraph. Which dialogue would make the best story starter? Circle that number.

C. Make a list of events to include in the paragraph. The events should be written in the order they will appear in the paragraph.

1. _____   3. _____

2. _____   4. _____

D. Write an opening paragraph with the dialogue you selected and the events from above. Put quotation marks at the beginning and end of each character's words.

_____

_____

_____

_____

Check Your Work

Does the dialogue make sense with the rest of the paragraph?

Whole Group Share your dialogue with the class.

Begin a Story with Dialogue

Dialogue is the exact words that a character is thinking or saying. Dialogue can be funny, serious, or inspirational. Starting a story with dialogue sparks the reader's interest.

Dialogue Words

whispered	screamed	exclaimed	announced	replied
laughed	screeched	yelled	explained	cried
answered	repeated	shouted	gasped	sighed

Dialogue Examples

"What was that?" the crowd gasped. Think — Did a spaceship just land?

I cried, "We're on our way!" Think — Are you going on vacation?

"Watch out," shouted the lifeguard. Think — Was there a shark in the ocean?

I exclaimed, "We have arrived!" Think — Did you want to be noticed?

Independently Begin a paragraph with dialogue.

A. Choose dialogue to begin a paragraph you will write. Use any dialogue of your choice or use dialogue from the examples above. Place quotation marks before and after what the character is saying.

_____

B. Why did you choose that dialogue?

I chose that dialogue because _____

_____ .

C. Write an opening paragraph beginning with the dialogue. Don't forget to put quotation marks before and after the exact words of the character.

_____

_____

_____

_____

Check Your Work

Will the dialogue get the attention of the reader?
Can you picture the character saying the dialogue?

Whole Group Share your dialogue with the class.

Begin a Story with a Teaser

This workbook was supposed to be about writing, but all I see are math problems. That's strange! Teasers are sentences that make people want to read more. They can be about things you would not expect to happen. When you open a writing book, you expect to see writing, not math. Strange and mysterious things are about to transpire in a story when you begin it with a teaser. Teasers have the reader wondering what will happen next.

Example: *Brandon was sure it was his house, but when he opened the door everything was different. He started to look around the house. Nothing looked the way he remembered it. What was going on?*

Whole Group As a group, we will practice using teasers.

Teasers

The swing was moving back and forth, but no one was on it.

Justin couldn't believe it.

Gabriella opened her backpack and found money.

A. Let's fill in each blank with the teaser from the list above that makes the best opener for each paragraph.

1. _____

He saw a squirrel up in the tree. It was wearing glasses and reading a book.

2. _____

Where did this come from? She couldn't imagine how it got in there.

3. _____

It wasn't the wind making it move. It was going higher and higher with each swing.

B. Can you find the teaser? Let's read the sentences and discuss why each sentence is or is not a teaser.

1. **I woke up and found myself alone in my classroom.**

2. **A computer is a great invention.**

3. **Mom drove my friends and me to the movies.**

4. **The sun was shining, even though it was 10 o'clock at night.**

Independently Write a teaser about an old, empty house. Did you hear or see something strange?

_____

_____

Whole Group Share your teaser with the class.

Begin a Story with a Teaser

Teasers are sentences that make people want to read more. They can be about things you would not expect to happen. The reader will wonder what will be revealed next.

Whole Group Let's write a teaser about seeing an elephant in an unusual place.

Brainstorming Time!

A. First, we will make a list of teasers that could be used in this situation. Think of strange or mysterious openers about the elephant. The teaser should surprise the reader because it is something unexpected.

1. _____

2. _____

3. _____

4. _____

B. Decide which teaser you think would make the best story opener. Why?
Vote for your favorite teaser.

The winning opening teaser is number _____ !

C. Next, we'll make a list of events to include in the paragraph. The events should be written in the order they will appear in the story.

1. _____   3. _____

2. _____   4. _____

D. Now, let's use the opening teaser and the list of events from Part C to complete the paragraph. Remember to be strange or mysterious.

_____

_____

_____

_____

_____

_____

> ## Check Your Work
>
> Is the teaser strange or mysterious?
>
> Will the reader be surprised by what happened in the paragraph?

Begin a Story with a Teaser

Teasers are sentences that make people want to read more. They can be about things you would not expect to happen. The reader will wonder what will be revealed next.

Partners With a partner, come up with details for teasers.

A. Fill in the blanks in the paragraph below by selecting an answer from each column. To fill in blank one, choose an answer from column one, and so on.

1	2	3	4	5
A bear	scary	try to help	the police	a rope
A puppy	yelping	hide from	a zookeeper	a cage
A horse	snorting	jump on	some children	hay
A dinosaur	crying	yell at	a cowboy	a camera

As I walked down the road, I couldn't believe what I saw. (1) _____
was coming toward me. It was (2) _____ and running as fast as it
could. I didn't know what to do. Should I (3) _____ it or just get out
of the way? Then I saw (4) _____ carrying (5) _____.
Suddenly, I heard, "Nicholas, get up for school!" Then I realized that it was only a
dream.

B. With your partner, write a teaser sentence for each of the following situations. Your teasers should be strange or mysterious.

1. Your snack is missing.

   _____

2. You see huge footprints.

   _____

Independently Write teasers for these situations.

1. Your coat changed colors.

   _____

2. Apple juice is coming out of the faucet.

   _____

┌───┐

Check Your Work

Are the teasers strange or mysterious?
Will the teasers surprise the reader?

└───┘

Whole Group Share your favorite teaser with the class.

Begin a Story with a Teaser

Teasers are sentences that make people want to read more. They can be about things you would not expect to happen. The reader will wonder what will be revealed next.

Independently Write an opening paragraph using the following teaser:

The door opened, but no one was there.

A. Think about the teaser. Why would the door open by itself? Write ideas for your paragraph. Make sure to think of something strange or mysterious.

1. _____

2. _____

3. _____

B. Select one of these ideas for your opening paragraph. Which idea would create the best story? The idea must also make sense with the teaser.

The idea that would make the best story is number _____ because _____

_____ .

C. Next, make a list of events to include in the paragraph. The events should be written in the order they will appear in the story.

1. _____   3. _____

2. _____   4. _____

D. Write an opening paragraph using the teaser and events above. The paragraph should be about something that is unexpected. Have the reader wondering what will happen later in the paragraph.

The door opened, but no one was there. _____

_____

_____

_____

_____

Check Your Work

Does your paragraph have the reader wondering what strange and mysterious thing will happen next?

Does the teaser make sense with the rest of the paragraph?

Whole Group Share your teaser with the class.

Begin a Story with a Teaser

Teasers are sentences that make people want to read more. They can be about things you would not expect to happen. Tickling the readers' curiosity will make them want to read on.

Independently Prepare to write an opening paragraph using any teaser of your choice or find a teaser from the list below.

Teasers

    a. All of a sudden the plant started growing a foot a minute.

    b. As I lay in bed, the creaking sound grew louder and louder.

    c. I couldn't believe what he was saying.

    d. You'll never guess what happened to me.

    e. The dog would not stop barking at the tree.

A. Decide what teaser you like best. Circle it.

B. Write ideas for your paragraph. Make sure to think of something strange or mysterious.

    1. _____

    2. _____

    3. _____

C. Decide which idea you will use for your paragraph. Make a list of events to include in the paragraph. The events should be written in the order they will appear in the story.

    1. _____   3. _____

    2. _____   4. _____

D. Write an opening paragraph using the teaser you chose and the events above. Make sure your teaser is strange or mysterious.

_____

_____

_____

_____

_____

> ## Check Your Work
> Does the teaser make the reader wonder what strange thing will happen?

Whole Group Share your teaser with the class.

Begin a Story with Setting

The setting of a story tells when and where the story takes place. Writers can use settings in order to set the mood. If the setting takes place in the deep, dark forest, the mood might be scary. Starting a paragraph with the setting helps the reader to visualize the character's surroundings and helps to develop the feel of the story.

Example: *At the park, Rebecca and Nicholas saw a little boy crying. He was sitting on a bench all by himself.*

A phrase is a group of words within a sentence that does not have a complete thought. *At the park* is a phrase. A preposition is a word that tells time or place. *At* is a preposition. You can begin a setting phrase with a preposition.

Prepositions

above	along	under	by	to	over
at	around	in	across	behind	before
below	on	against	between	up	about

Whole Group As a group, we will use setting in an opening sentence.

A. Let's fill in the blanks with a word from the list to complete each phrase. The phrase will tell information about the setting.

1. _____ the road, there were wildflowers growing.

2. _____ the girls, stood an angry friend.

3. _____ the corner, I could see my dad waiting for me.

4. _____ breakfast, I had a long talk with my grandmother.

B. Write phrases using the words below. Start each phrase with a word from the box.

1. **city:** _____

2. **house:** _____

3. **bridge:** _____

Independently Write opening sentences beginning with the phrases you helped create. The openers should place the reader immediately in the story.
Rule: Always place a comma after the opening phrase.

1. _____

2. _____

3. _____

Whole Group Share your favorite sentence with the class.

Begin a Story with Setting

The setting of a story tells when and where the story takes place. Writers can use settings in order to set the mood. Starting a paragraph with the setting helps the reader to visualize the character's surroundings and helps to develop the feel of the story. Using a setting as an opener immediately places the reader in the story.

Remember: A preposition is a word that tells time or place.

Prepositions

above	beneath	under	by	to	over
at	around	in	across	behind	before
below	on	against	between	up	about

Whole Group Let's write an opening paragraph using setting.

Brainstorming Time!

A. First, we will make a list of phrases. Begin each phrase with a preposition from the list.

1. _____   3. _____

2. _____   4. _____

B. Next, let's write opening sentences for two of the phrases. Remember to place a comma after the opening phrase.

1. _____

2. _____

C. Which setting opener do you think would make the best story? Vote for your favorite opening sentence.

The winning opening sentence is number _____ !

D. Now we'll complete the paragraph.

_____

_____

_____

_____

Check Your Work

Did you put a comma after the opening phrase?

Can you visualize when or where the story is taking place?

Begin a Story with Setting

Writers use settings to open stories in order to set the mood. Starting a paragraph with the setting helps the reader to visualize the character's surroundings. Using a setting as an opener immediately places the reader in the story.

Partners   In pairs, learn about prepositions with riddles.

Remember: A preposition is a word that tells time or place.

Prepositions					
above	beneath	under	by	after	over
at	around	in	across	behind	before
below	on	against	between	up	about

A. Solve each riddle. Use a preposition from the list.

1. It is made of steel.

   I hear cars driving above me.

   I see a river flowing below it.

   Where am I?

   I am_____ .

2. There is a rainbow in the sky.

   The ground is wet.

   There are large puddles everywhere.

   When is it?

   It is _____ .

B. Write a riddle. The riddle should include three clues and a question to answer. The answer must be a phrase that starts with a preposition.

_____
(clue)

_____
(clue)

_____
(clue)

_____
(question)

_____
(answer)

Check Your Work

Does the answer start with a preposition?

Whole Group Volunteer to share your riddle with the class.

Begin a Story with Setting

The setting of a story tells when and where the story takes place. Writers use settings to open stories in order to set the mood and to place the reader immediately in the story.

Independently Write a paragraph with a setting opener.

A. Write opening sentences starting with settings. Begin the sentences using the following phrases.

1. Against the brick wall, _____ .

2. On the mountain, _____ .

3. Before the game, _____ .

4. Into the starry night, _____ .

5. At the museum, _____ .

B. Select one of these sentences for the opening paragraph you are going to write.

C. Make a list of events to include in the paragraph. The events should be written in the order they will appear in the paragraph.

1. _____   3. _____

2. _____   4. _____

D. Write an opening paragraph with the setting opener you selected and the events above. By starting the paragraph with a setting, you can help the reader visualize the character's surroundings and understand the mood of the story.

_____

_____

_____

_____

_____

_____

Check Your Work
Does the opener place the reader in the story?
Did you use prepositions anywhere else in the paragraph?

Whole Group Share your opening sentence with the class.

Begin a Story with Setting

The setting of a story tells when and where the story takes place. Writers use settings to open stories in order to set the mood and to place the reader immediately in the story.

Remember: A preposition is a word that tells time or place.

Prepositions

above	beneath	under	by	to	over
at	around	in	across	behind	before
below	on	against	between	up	about

Opening Sentences

After the carnival, Kubair and his friends decided to walk home.
Beyond the parking lot, Alexis saw the finish line.
During the test, the fire alarm started to blare.
Beneath my bed, I saw something strange.

Independently Write an opening paragraph using a setting sentence.

A. Choose a setting opener from the box or create one to begin your paragraph.

_____

B. Make a list of events to include in the paragraph. The events should be written in the order they will appear in the paragraph.

1. _____   3. _____

2. _____   4. _____

C. Write an opening paragraph with the setting opener and the events from above. The opening sentence should place the reader immediately in the story.

_____

_____

_____

_____

Check Your Work

Can you visualize the character in the setting?

Does the setting create a mood for the reader?

Whole Group Share your opening sentence with the class.

Connect Beginning Ideas

Writers use transitional words or phrases to connect ideas. *First of all*, *in the beginning*, and *now* are examples of transitions that can be used to begin a new paragraph. In the following example, notice how the ideas in the opening paragraph flow into the next one because of transitional words and phrases.

Example

What made me think that I could bake a cake? Baking a cake was a bad idea. It looks like it was run over by a truck. No one will ever want to eat this disgusting looking thing.

   First of all, *I left out the baking powder. I could tell the minute I saw it. The cake came out of the oven as flat as a pancake . . .*

Beginning Transitional Words and Phrases

first	to start with	now	originally
first of all	to begin with	once	for one thing
at first	in the beginning	initially	before
in the first place	immediately	one time	at present

Whole Group Let's start each of the following sentences with a transitional word or phrase from the above list. The transition must make sense with the rest of the sentence.

1. _____ , we had planned to go to the beach, but it rained.

2. _____ , having a class pet seemed like a good idea, until we had to clean the cage.

3. _____ , you need to have all the supplies necessary to decorate an aquarium.

4. _____ , I only have one dog, but I am planning on getting another dog for my birthday.

Independently Write a transitional word or phrase from the list above to begin each sentence. The transition must make sense with the rest of the sentence.

1. _____ , Angelina wrote a play that she also performed in front of the class.

2. _____ , everything seemed easy, until I discovered a big problem with the assignment.

3. _____ , making the graph showed me how much junk food the class ate in one day.

Whole Group Share one of the sentences with the class.

Connect Beginning Ideas

Transitional words are used at the beginning of the second paragraph to connect the opening paragraph to the events that follow. A writer can use transitional words and phrases at the beginning of a paragraph to make ideas flow from one paragraph to the next.

Beginning Transitional Words and Phrases

first	to start with	now	originally
first of all	to begin with	once	for one thing
at first	in the beginning	initially	before
in the first place	immediately	one time	at present

Whole Group As a group, we will write using transitional words and phrases.

A. Let's read the following paragraphs.

"Mom, get this kid away from me!" screamed Megan. She had a million things to do before the party, and her little brother would not stop bothering her. She was really getting nervous. Megan didn't think she would ever be ready.

_____ *, Megan had to finish putting up all the decorations . . .*

B. The beginning sentence of the second paragraph is missing a transitional word or phrase. As a group, list transitional words or phrases that could fill in the blank.

1. _____
2. _____
3. _____
4. _____

C. Think about the transitions. Vote for your favorite transitional word or phrase.

The winning number is _____ !

D. Next, let's make a list of events to include in the second paragraph. The events should be written in the order they will appear in the paragraph.

1. _____
2. _____
3. _____
4. _____

E. Now, we'll complete the second paragraph. First, fill in the blank with the winning transition. Then include the events above to complete the paragraph

_____ *, Megan had to finish putting up all the decorations.*

_____

_____

Check Your Work

Does the transition make the ideas flow from one paragraph to the next?

Connect Beginning Ideas

Transitional words and phrases are used at the beginning of the second paragraph to connect the opening paragraph to the events that follow. Transitions show the sequence in a story, enabling the reader to follow and make sense of the events. The ideas will move along in a logical order when you use transitional words and phrases.

Transitional Words and Phrases that Show Sequence

first	soon	in closing
first of all	next	in the end
in the beginning	after that	in conclusion
to start with	at last	finally

Partners In pairs, use transitional words and phrases to show sequence.

A. Each set of sentences below is in the wrong sequence. With a partner, number the sentences from 1 to 3 to put them into the correct order. Then choose a transitional word or phrase from each list to indicate the sequence.

Order   Transitions

_____ _____ , the boy was riding his bike.

_____ _____ , he went home, and his mom bandaged his knee.

_____ _____ , he fell off his bike and hurt his knee.

_____ _____ , he was nervous that he would make a mistake.

_____ _____ , the audience loved Kyle's performance.

_____ _____ , Kyle practiced every day for his recital.

B. Now write a paragraph using transitional words and phrases that shows sequence. Your paragraph should include the three steps needed to make a sandwich. Remember to include three transitional words or phrases.

_____

_____

_____

_____

Check Your Work

Does the paragraph include transitional words to sequence the story?

Whole Group Share your paragraph with the class.

Connect Beginning Ideas

Writers use transitional words and phrases at the beginning of a paragraph to make ideas flow from one paragraph to the next. Transitional words and phrases are used at the beginning of the second paragraph to connect the opening paragraph to the events that follow.

Beginning Transitional Words and Phrases

first	to start with	now	originally
first of all	to begin with	once	for one thing
at first	in the beginning	initially	before

Independently Use a beginning transition in a second paragraph.

A. Read the opening paragraph.

"I'll never get this room clean," sighed Samantha to herself. Samantha had promised her mother that her bedroom would be clean and neat before she left for her soccer game. As she looked around the room and saw the big piles of her things, Samantha knew she had to work fast in order to keep her promise.

B. Use the beginning transitional words and phrases below to complete possible beginning sentences for the second paragraph. The sentences should make sense with the opening paragraph about Samantha's room.

1. First, _____

2. To begin with, _____

C. Select one of the above sentences to begin the second paragraph of the story.

D. Make a list of events to include in the paragraph. The events should be written in the order they will appear in the paragraph.

1. _____ 3. _____

2. _____ 4. _____

E. Write the second paragraph with the sentence you selected and the events you listed. Make sure this paragraph flows smoothly from the opening paragraph.

_____

_____

_____

Check Your Work
Does your story flow from one paragraph to the next?

Whole Group Share your transition sentence with the class.

Connect Beginning Ideas

Transitional words and phrases are used at the beginning of the second paragraph to connect the opening paragraph to the events that follow. Transitions show the sequence in a story, enabling the reader to follow and make sense of the events.

Beginning Transitional Words and Phrases

first	to start with	now	originally
first of all	to begin with	once	for one thing
at first	in the beginning	initially	before

Independently Write a second paragraph with a transition.

A. Read the opening paragraph. Then think about what could happen next.

Bam! Brandon threw his textbooks on the table. In class that day, his teacher had assigned a five-page, typed report. The worst part about the whole thing was that it was due the following Friday.

B. Choose a transitional word or phrase to begin the next paragraph and write it here. Use the list of beginning transitional words to help you.

_____

D. Make a list of events to include in the paragraph. The events should be written in the order they will appear in the paragraph.

1. _____   3. _____

2. _____   4. _____

E. Write the second paragraph beginning with the sentence that you chose and the events you listed.

_____

_____

_____

_____

_____

_____

Check Your Work
Are your ideas flowing from one paragraph to the next?

Whole Group Share your transition sentence with the class.

Add Transitions to Continue Ideas

A writer can use transitional words and phrases at the beginning of the second paragraph to connect the opening paragraph to the events that follow. Transitional words and phrases are also written in the following paragraphs to continue to bridge ideas. Using transitional words and phrases in the middle of the story will improve connections.

Transitional Words and Phrases

then	since	however	for example
second	instead of	although	rather than
next	otherwise	afterward	even though
besides	also	especially	usually

Whole Group As a group, read the story and practice using transitions.

A. Let's read the following paragraphs. Notice how the ideas in the opening paragraph flow into the second paragraph and then on to the third with transitional words and phrases. Beginning the third paragraph with the word *after* helps the reader follow the sequence of the story.

> *What made me think that I could bake a cake? Baking a cake was a bad idea. It looks like it was run over by a truck.*

> ***First of all,*** *I left out the baking powder. I could tell the minute I saw it. The cake came out of the oven as flat as a pancake.*

> ***After*** *my baking disaster, I decided to go to the bakery to buy a cake. I thought that was good idea. However, when I got there, the only cake that was left had "Happy Birthday" written on it. What should I do?*

B. Now, we'll start each of the following sentences with a transitional word or phrase from the above list. The transition must make sense with the rest of the sentence.

1. _____ my brother never studies, he always gets high grades.

2. _____, I went to the movies and bought popcorn and a soda.

3. _____ going to the mall, we went skating.

Independently Write a transitional word or phrase from the list above to begin each sentence.

1. _____, I do my homework when I get home from school.

2. _____, Jordan is always kind and considerate of others.

3. _____, my parents told us we were going on vacation.

Whole Group Share a sentence with the transition you added.

Add Transitions to Continue Ideas

Transitional words and phrases are used to connect ideas from one paragraph to another. Transitions show sequence and time in a paragraph. Using transitional words and phrases in the middle of the story will connect ideas to help the story move forward.

Transitional Words and Phrases

then	since	however	finally
second	usually	although	afterward

Whole Group Continue a story with transitional words and phrases.

A. Let's read the paragraphs. Notice how the ideas in the opening paragraph flow into the second paragraph because of the transition word "now."

Ding, dong! It must be my first guest. I open the door, and Susan is standing there holding her sleeping bag in one hand and her teddy bear in the other. Behind her I see Sherry running up the sidewalk waving her latest CD. We will be dancing all night.

***Now,** we are just waiting for Marie to arrive and the party can really begin. While we wait, everyone finds the perfect spot for their sleeping bag and dives into the snacks. Sherry puts on the music and turns up the volume. Amazingly, we hear the doorbell.*

_____ *Marie runs into the room screaming, "I'm here!"*

Brainstorming Time!

B. The last sentence in the story above is missing a transitional word or phrase. Let's come up with a transitional word or phrase that could be used in the blank above.

_____

C. Next, we'll make a list of events to include in the paragraph. The events should be written in the order they will appear in the paragraph.

1. _____   3. _____

2. _____   4. _____

D. Let's complete the third paragraph. Fill in the blank with the winning transition and include the events from Part C.

_____ Marie runs into the room screaming, "I'm here!"

_____

_____

_____

Check Your Work

Does the transition make the ideas flow from one paragraph to the next?

Add Transitions to Continue Ideas

Transitional words and phrases can be used between sentences, paragraphs, or entire sections of work to show sequence and connect ideas.

Transitional Words and Phrases

meanwhile	after that	soon	then	before
long	later on	afterwards	earlier	still
later	an hour later	next	shortly	after
eventually	as soon as	shortly	at first	finally

Partners   With a partner, use transitional words to connect two simple sentences in different ways.

A. Fill in the blanks in each set of sentences with different transition words. Add punctuation as needed.

Example: *Christopher did his homework _____ he went out to play.*
Christopher did his homework; without delay, he went out to play.
Christopher did his homework. Afterwards, he went out to play.

1. We started to pet the puppy _____ it wagged its tail.

   We started to pet the puppy _____ it wagged its tail.

2. Dad said I couldn't go to the mall _____ he changed his mind.

   Dad said I couldn't go to the mall _____ he changed his mind.

3. I got ready for the movie _____ my mom drove me to the theater.

   I got ready for the movie _____ my mom drove me to the theater.

B. Write two simple sentences that can be connected with transitions. Link the sentences by adding transitional words or phrases. You can use the list of transitions to help you.

   1. _____

      _____

   2. _____

      _____

Check Your Work

Can you think of another way to write the sentences using transitions?

Whole Group Share one of your sentences with the class.

Add Transitions to Continue Ideas

Transitional words and phrases move ideas along in a logical order. Transitions can be written in the middle of the story to bridge ideas and to tell when things are happening.

Independently Continue the story below using transitional words and phrases.

Transitional Words and Phrases

then	since	however	earlier	second
eventually	although	rather than	next	later
as soon as	after that	besides	still	later on
an hour later	meanwhile	shortly after	soon	afterwards

A. Read the following paragraphs.

I didn't take this picture! How did it get on my camera? As I looked at the pictures I had taken at the zoo, I saw one of a strange creature. It was as big as a grizzly bear, but it had green fur and a tail like a kangaroo.

Initially, I was really frightened and confused. My imagination was going wild. I even thought that maybe I had been abducted by aliens.

B. Using the transitional words and phrases above, write two sentences that could begin the third paragraph. Each sentence should make sense with the other paragraphs.

1. _____

2. _____

C. Select one of the above sentences to begin the third paragraph. Then, make a list of events to include in the paragraph. The events should be written in the order they will appear in the paragraph.

1. _____   3. _____

2. _____   4. _____

D. Write the third paragraph with the sentence you selected and the events you listed. Make sure this paragraph flows smoothly from the second paragraph.

_____

_____

_____

Check Your Work
Does the sentence you selected help the reader follow the story?

Whole Group Share your transition sentence with the class.

Add Transitions to Continue Ideas

Transitional words and phrases are used to connect ideas from one paragraph to another. Transitions show sequence and time in a paragraph.

Transitional Sentences

Since it was the day of the game, I knew I had to do my best.

After that practice, I thought I would be a disaster on the field.

Then I began to get my confidence back.

Afterwards, I decided to go to the field and practice some more.

Shortly after that practice, I talked to my coach.

Independently Use transitions to continue the story below.

A. Read the paragraphs. Think about what could happen next.

Did you ever want something so badly that it was all you could think about? That was the way I felt about getting on the hockey team. Every minute of the day I dreamed about it. I was the happiest kid ever when I made the team.

In the beginning, it was amazing. I liked my team, so I was having a great time. Everything was perfect, until I found out that our first game was on Saturday. I was so nervous and scared that at practice I couldn't do anything right.

B. Choose the best transition from the box to begin the third paragraph. Write it here.

_____

C. Make a list of events to include in the paragraph. The events should be written in the order they will appear in the paragraph.

1. _____   3. _____

2. _____   4. _____

D. Write the third paragraph beginning with the transitional sentence that you chose and the events you listed. Glue your ideas together with more transitions if needed.

_____

_____

_____

Check Your Work

Are your ideas flowing from one paragraph to the next?

Whole Group Share your transition sentence with the class.

Add Transitions to End a Story

Writers use transitional words and phrases throughout their stories. Transitions help to move and connect ideas throughout the story. *Finally*, *in conclusion*, and *as a result* are examples of transitions that are used at the end of a story. These transitions bring the events to an understandable and meaningful conclusion.

Example

What made me think that I could bake a cake? Baking a cake was a bad idea. It looks like it was run over by a truck. No one will ever want to eat this!

First of all, *I left out the baking powder. I could tell the minute I saw it. The cake came out of the oven as flat as a pancake.*

After *my baking disaster, I decided to go to the bakery to buy a cake. However, when I got there, the only cake that was left had "Happy Birthday" written on it.*

In the end, *I asked the baker to change the message on the cake from "Happy Birthday" to "Happy Anniversary." To my surprise he said, "Yes!" What a relief! Most importantly, my parents are going to have a wonderful anniversary.*

Ending Transitional Words and Phrases

in conclusion	finally	as a result	consequently
accordingly	thereafter	basically	with this in mind
in other words	lastly	at last	most importantly
for this reason	in the end	in closing	from that time on

Whole Group Let's start each of the following sentences with a transitional word or phrase from the above list. The transition we choose must make sense. Keep in mind that they are all concluding sentences.

1. _____, Jonathan missed the bus and was late for school.

2. _____, my brother will always keep his promises.

3. _____, Richard found his lost key.

4. _____, the class decided to donate money to save endangered animals.

Independently Write a transitional word or phrase from the list above to begin each sentence. The transition must make sense with the rest of each concluding sentence.

1. _____, Justin considered that maybe he was wrong.

2. _____, the play was a huge success.

Whole Group Share one of the sentences with the class.

Add Transitions to End a Story

Transitional words and phrases move and connect ideas throughout a story. Transitions link earlier events to later ones and then to the ending in a meaningful and logical way.

Ending Transitional Words and Phrases

in conclusion	finally	as a result	consequently
for this reason	in the end	basically	with this in mind
in other words	lastly	at last	most importantly

Whole Group Let's make an ending for the story below with transitional words and phrases.

    *"Hurray!" yelled Nicole excitedly. **Today,** Nicole and her family were leaving for a vacation. She couldn't wait. Nicole didn't expect what was about to happen.*

    ***To start with,** her parents' alarm clock didn't go off on time. Everyone was rushing around like crazy to get ready. They quickly got dressed and packed all their suitcases in the car for the drive to the airport.*

    ***Before long,** Nicole's family was at the airport. Soon, they were running with their suitcases to have them checked.*

    _____ *, Nicole and her family got on the plane.*

Brainstorming Time!

A. The beginning sentence of the last paragraph is missing a transitional word or phrase. Lets write a word or phrase that will work with the sentence

_____

B. Next, we'll make a list of events to include in the paragraph. The events should be written in the order they will appear in the paragraph.

    1. _____   3. _____

    2. _____   4. _____

C. Let's continue working together to complete the final paragraph. Fill in the blank with the transition you chose and include the events you listed.

_____ , Nicole and her family got on the plane.

_____

_____

_____

Add Transitions to End a Story

Transitional words and phrases show sequence and connect ideas in all types of writing. Transitions are especially useful when writing the steps to do a task.

Partners With a partner, circle all the transitional words and phrases in the how-to paragraph below.

How to Set a Table

Setting a table is easy when you know the proper place for everything. First, learn where everything should be placed on the table. When you have all the plates, forks, spoons, knives, and napkins you need for each place setting, you are ready to begin.

To start with, put a plate on the table for each person who will be eating. Second, fold the napkins in half. Then place the napkins on the right side of the plate.

After that, put the knife on the napkin close to the plate with the blade facing in. The next thing you need to do is to get the spoon and place it to the right of the knife.

Finally, lay the fork on the left side of the plate. This is the last step you need to do. Now, you are ready to eat. Enjoy!

Whole Group As a group, review and list the transitional words and phrases you circled.

_____

_____

_____

Partners Now, in pairs, fill in the blanks in the how-to story about making chocolate milk. Make sure the reader can follow the sequence of the story.

Almost everyone loves to drink chocolate milk. In order to make chocolate milk you need to do the following steps. _____ , get the milk from the refrigerator. _____ , find a glass and pour in the milk. Do not fill the milk to the top of the glass because you need room for the chocolate syrup.

_____ , measure a tablespoon of chocolate syrup. _____ , put the spoonful of syrup into the glass of milk. _____ , stir the milk and chocolate syrup together, until they are completely mixed. You are done! _____ , it's time to drink your delicious chocolate milk.

> ## Check Your Work
>
> Do the transitions make the story flow from beginning to end?

Whole Group Volunteer to share your how-to story with the class.

Add Transitions to End a Story

Transitional words and phrases move ideas along in a logical order to the end. Transitions help the reader understand the story.

Independently End the story below with transitional words and phrases.

Where were my cleats? The soccer game was starting in five minutes, and I couldn't find them in my bag. I had been riding in the car for an hour to get to the game. There was no way that I could go home to get them. My dad was not going to be happy.

In the first place, I should have checked to make sure I had everything I needed for the game. This was not the first time I had forgotten something. I did it all the time.

At that moment, I didn't have a choice. I had to tell my dad that I had forgotten my cleats. Oh no! Here he came. "Dad, I have something to tell you," I mumbled.

A. Using the transitional words and phrases below, complete each sentence for the beginning of the last paragraph. Each sentence should make sense with the other paragraphs about the forgetful soccer player.

1. Thereafter, _____

2. As a result, _____

3. From that time on, _____

B. Select one of the above sentences to begin the last paragraph. Circle the number.

C. Make a list of events to include in the closing paragraph. The events should be written in the order they will appear in the paragraph.

1. _____   3. _____

2. _____   4. _____

D. Write the closing paragraph with the sentence you selected and the events you listed.

_____

_____

_____

_____

_____

Check Your Work
Does the ending connect the ideas and resolve the problem?

Whole Group Share your transition with the class.

Add Transitions to End a Story

Writers connect ideas from the beginning paragraph to the end by using transitional words and phrases. Transitions bring all the events of a story to an understandable conclusion.

Whole Group Read the paragraphs. Think of how the story could end.

"These boots are awesome!" I exclaimed. "They are just what I wanted. I didn't think Mom knew what I liked. I guess Mom is cooler than I thought."

I remember that one time Mom bought me a shirt for my birthday. It was the ugliest thing I had ever seen. Luckily, Mom told me I could take it back.

After that, Mom started letting me pick out my own clothes. She rarely buys me anything without me being there. I was really surprised when I got the boots.

Independently Write the last paragraph, starting it with a transitional sentence.

Transitional Sentences

In closing, I am going to remember that Mom tries hard to please me.

In the end, I realized that Mom doesn't have the worst taste in the world.

In other words, I am lucky to have such a great mom.

Most importantly, Mom really loves me.

Lastly, Mom is pretty cool.

A. Write the sentence you will use to begin the last paragraph.

_____

B. Make a list of events to include in the last paragraph. The events should be written in the order they will appear.

1. _____   3. _____

2. _____   4. _____

C. Write the closing paragraph, beginning with the sentence that you chose and the events you listed.

_____

_____

_____

_____

Check Your Work

Do the ideas flow from the first paragraph to the closing?

Whole Group Share your transition with the class.

Close a Story with a Memory

Remember a special time you had with your friends. Why do you remember this time? You don't remember every day of your life, but you do remember special and important events. Ending a story with a memory shows the reader that the event being remembered is significant.

> **Example:** *The girl sighed as she thought about how close she had come to losing the championship game. What a relief! She knew she would never forget that day as long as she lived.*

Memory Words and Phrases

always remember	recall	never forget	reminds me	memorable
remember	remind	brings to mind	unforgettable	looking back

Memory Closings

I had an unforgettable day with my friends.   I will never forget how funny he was.

Looking back, I should have remembered the time I was scared by a big kid.

Whole Group Let's fill in the blanks with the memory closings above.

1. At last, my family decided on a name for our new kitten. We saw him covered in peanut butter and licking his mouth. We knew what we had to call him: "Peanut!" _____

   _____

2. As a result of the rainy weather, we could not go to the beach. I thought it would be a terrible day, but I was wrong. I was allowed to invite some of my friends over, and we pretended to be famous movie stars on our own show. _____

3. Lastly, it is fun to dress up in scary costumes on Halloween. Being a vampire was so cool, but I guess I should not have scared all the little children in the neighborhood. They actually thought I was real. Now I feel like a big bully. _____

   _____

Independently Write your own memory closing for one of the paragraphs above. Use the list of memory words and phrases to help you.

_____

Whole Group Share your memory closing with the class.

Close a Story with a Memory

Writers end a story with a memory to remind the reader of special events or to show the importance of certain events.

Whole Group We will write an ending with a memory.

Memory Words and Phrases

always remember	recall	never forget	reminds me
looking back	remind	brings to mind	think of
memorable	unforgettable	call to mind	remember

A. Let's read the ending paragraph. It is missing a closing sentence.

> *From that time on, Marie had more confidence in herself. She realized that she had a lot of great ideas and could do as well as anyone else.*

Let's create a list of closing sentences that include a memory. When using words and phrases from the list above, we may change the verb's tense if needed.

1. _____

2. _____

3. _____

Time to Practice!

B. Have you ever been caught outside in a rainstorm? As a group, we'll write a closing paragraph about a rainstorm. First, we'll make a list of events to include.

1. _____   3. _____

2. _____   4. _____

C. Next, let's write a memory closing that would make sense with the events you listed.

_____

D. Now, we'll write the closing paragraph. Use the events you listed and the memory closing you wrote.

_____

_____

_____

Check Your Work

Is the ending sentence memorable?

Close a Story with a Memory

People sometimes keep a record of important events in their lives by writing in a diary or journal every day. Writing in diaries helps people to save their memories in a special place. Writing in a diary is like writing a letter to someone who will keep all your secrets and thoughts. To the right is an entry in a diary written by a fictional character, Lily, who has just tried out for the basketball team.

> *November 19*
>
> *Dear Diary,*
> *This was an exciting day. I tried out for the basketball team. I was one of the shortest people who tried out, but I made some great shots. I hope I was good enough to make the team. I will find out soon.*
>
> *Good night,*
> *Lily*

Partners   In pairs, pretend to be Lily and write the next diary entry.

November 20

Dear Diary,

_____

_____

_____

_____
(closing)

Lily

Independently Write your own diary entry for today. Did anything special happen to you? What memory do you want to keep in your diary?

_____
(date)

Dear Diary,

_____

_____

_____

_____

_____
(closing)

_____
(signature)

Whole Group Volunteer to share one of the diary entries with the class.

Close a Story with a Memory

A writer can end a story with a memory to remind the reader of special events or to show the importance of certain events.

Independently Write an ending with a memory.

Memory Words and Phrases

always remember	recall	never forget	reminds me
looking back	remind	brings to mind	think of
memorable	unforgettable	call to mind	remember

A. Fill in each blank with a memory word or phrase from the above list.

1. This hiking trip was a/an _____ experience.

2. I will _____ how I felt that day.

3. Today _____ the time my sister won her first race.

4. Julia will always _____ the spelling bee and feel proud.

B. Select one of the above memory closings for a paragraph. Which memory closing would make the best ending?

The memory closing that would make the best ending is number _____ because _____.

C. Now make a list of events to include in the paragraph. The events should be written in the order they will happen in the paragraph.

1. _____   3. _____

2. _____   4. _____

D. Write an ending paragraph with the memory closing and events you listed. Remember to begin your closing paragraph with a transitional word or phrase, such as *finally*, *at last*, *in conclusion*, or *in the end*.

_____

_____

_____

_____

Check Your Work

Is the closing memorable?

Whole Group Share your memory closing with the class.

Close a Story with a Memory

A writer can end a story with a memory to remind the reader of important earlier events. The reader will have a lasting impression of the story when it ends with a memory.

Memory Words and Phrases

always remember	recall	never forget	reminds me
looking back	remind	brings to mind	think of
memorable	unforgettable	call to mind	remember

Memory Closings

What happened today will always remind me of how lucky I am.

Being chosen to be the captain of my team was very memorable.

It was an unforgettable day at the amusement park.

I will always remember the time I hit a home run to win the game.

Crystal will have a wonderful memory of her first day of school.

Independently Write a closing paragraph, ending it with a memory. You may use any of the memory closings above or write your own using the list of memory words and phrases. The closing should be about something special and memorable.

A. Write the memory closing sentence for your paragraph.

_____

B. Now make a list of events to include in the paragraph. The events should be written in the order they will happen in the paragraph.

1. _____   3. _____

2. _____   4. _____

C. Write an ending paragraph with the memory closing and events you wrote above. Remember to begin with a transitional word or phrase, such as *finally*, *at last*, *in conclusion*, or *in the end*.

_____

_____

_____

_____

Check Your Work

Will the ending be memorable?

Whole Group Share your memory closing with the class.

Close a Story with a Decision

Make a choice. It could be a choice between right and wrong, whether or not to try something new, or what outfit you should buy. People are always making decisions. A writer can end a story with a decision based on a lesson that was learned. A decision at the end of a story gives the reader a chance to agree or disagree with the choice that was made.

Example: *Finally, I followed the horrible smell. It was coming from my closet. I kept sniffing and discovered it was my backpack. I unzipped it and looked inside. There I found a half-eaten sandwich. It was moldy and rotten. YUCK! From now on, I am going to clean out my backpack every day.*

Decision Words and Phrases

resolve	made up my mind	determine	after what happened
this time	because of that	I will never	from now on
concluded	therefore, I decided	I will always	as a result

Whole Group Let's write decision closings for each paragraph, using words and phrases from the box above.

1. Last month, I promised my parents I would take care of the flower garden. I was going to weed it every week and water it daily in order to earn more money for a new game. Looking at the garden, I knew my parents would be able to tell that I did not keep my promise. Almost all of the flowers were dead or drooping. _____

    _____

2. At last, the parade was over. It was the first time I had ever marched in one. I thought it was really exciting. I was waving at everyone as I fooled around with my baseball team. Everything was going great, until I bumped into the person in front of me and made him fall. _____

    _____

3. Basically, I waited until the last minute to tell my dad I had to sell candy bars for my bicycle club. Now, I have fifty candy bars to sell in two days. _____

    _____

Independently Write your own decision closing for one of the paragraphs above. Use the list of decision words and phrases to help you.

_____

_____

Whole Group Share your decision closing with the class.

Close a Story with a Decision

A writer can end a story with a decision that the character has made. A decision at the end of a story gives the reader a chance to agree or disagree with the choice that was made.

Whole Group We will write an ending with a decision.

Decision Words and Phrases

resolve	made up my mind	determine	after what happened
this time	because of that	I will never	from now on
concluded	therefore, I decided	I will always	as a result

A. Let's read the ending paragraph. It is missing a closing sentence.

> *At last, I heard the news that I was waiting for. School will be closed due to blizzard. I am excited to have the day off! There are so many things I want to do.*

Think of how you feel when you get a day off from school. Let's create three decision sentences that could be used to end the paragraph above.

1. _____

2. _____

3. _____

Time to Practice!

B. Have you ever lost your homework? We will write a closing paragraph about losing homework. First, let's make a list of events to include in the closing paragraph.

1. _____   3. _____

2. _____   4. _____

C. Next, let's write a decision closing that would make sense with the events above.

_____

D. Now, we will write the closing paragraph. Use the events and decision closing above. Start the paragraph with an ending transitional word or phrase.

_____

_____

_____

_____

Check Your Work

Does the ending sentence make a good decision?

Close a Story with a Decision

A writer can end a story with a decision that the main character has made. People make decisions every day. Some decisions are good, and some are bad.

Partners With your partner, read the problems that the characters are experiencing. Then write three possible solutions for each one. Pick the solution you think is the best for each problem. Then write why you think that is the best solution.

Your best friend wants you to go skating, but you have a test to study for.

1. _____

2. _____

3. _____

The best solution is _____ because _____ .

You have soccer practice to go to, but you have a lot of homework to do.

1. _____

2. _____

3. _____

The best solution is _____ because _____ .

You got money for your birthday and you want to buy a toy, but you would have to spend all the money. Your parents said you should save some of the money.

1. _____

2. _____

3. _____

The best solution is _____ because _____ .

There is one piece of cake left and you really want to eat it, but you have already eaten more than your share.

1. _____

2. _____

3. _____

The best solution is _____ because _____ .

Check Your Work

Did you make good decisions with your partner?

Whole Group Share one best solution with the class.

Close a Story with a Decision

A writer can end a story with a decision that the character has made. A decision at the end of a story gives the reader a chance to agree or disagree with the choice that was made.

Decision Words and Phrases

resolve	made up my mind	determine	after what happened
this time	because of that	I will never	from now on
concluded	therefore, I decided	I will always	as a result

Independently Write a paragraph using a decision word or phrase.

A. Fill in each blank with a decision word or phrase from the above list. One of these sentences will be used as a decision closing.

1. _____ Steve let his little brother play with his friends.

2. _____ I will study harder for a test.

3. I _____ I will never go play without permission again.

B. Select one of the above decision closings for a paragraph. Circle that number.

C. Now make a list of events to include in the paragraph. The events should be written in the order they will happen in the paragraph.

1. _____   3. _____

2. _____   4. _____

D. Write an ending paragraph with the decision closing you selected. Use the events you listed to complete the paragraph. Remember to begin your closing paragraph with a transitional word or phrase, such as *finally*, *at last*, *in conclusion*, or *in the end*.

_____

_____

_____

_____

Check Your Work

Does the closing make the reader think about the decision that was made?

Did you remember to begin your closing paragraph with a transitional word or phrase?

Whole Group Share your decision closing with the class.

Close a Story with a Decision

A writer can end a story with a decision based on a lesson that was learned. A decision at the end of a story gives the reader a chance to agree or disagree with the choice that was made.

Independently Write a closing paragraph that ends with a decision. You may write your own using the list of decision words and phrases or use any of the decision closings below.

Decision Words and Phrases

resolve	made up my mind	this time	after what happened
determine	because of that	I will never	from now on
concluded	therefore, I decided	I will always	as a result

Decision Closings

Therefore, I decided to play soccer instead of hockey…

Richard made up his mind to throw away the things he did not need…

From now on, Helen will listen to her teacher…

A. Write the decision closing for your paragraph.

_____

Why do you think this is the best decision closing?

I think this is the best closing because _____ .

B. Now make a list of events to include in the paragraph. The events should be written in the order they will happen in the paragraph.

1. _____   3. _____

2. _____   4. _____

C. Write an ending paragraph with the decision closing you chose and the events you listed. Remember to begin your closing paragraph with a transitional word or phrase, such as *finally*, *at last*, *in conclusion*, or *in the end*.

_____

_____

_____

_____

Check Your Work

Did you remember to begin your closing paragraph with a transitional word or phrase?

Whole Group Share your decision closing with the class.

Close a Story with a Wish

I wish I had a million dollars. POOF! Oh, rats! I only got five! Not all wishes come true, but it is fun to dream about them. When you make a wish, you hope that something wonderful will happen. A writer can choose to end a story with a wish so the character can look forward to something special in the future. A wish at the closing of a story has the reader looking forward to a happy ending.

Wish Words and Phrases

my dream	I wish	hopefully	I want	in my daydreams
I hope I get	if only I	I am hopeful	imagine	look forward to
wish for	I hope	my desire	I intend	with any luck

Wish Closings

He hoped that tomorrow would be a better day.
I wish I could have stayed longer.
Hopefully, everyone will agree and the party will be great.

Whole Group Let's give each of these closing paragraphs an ending that is a wish or hope. Fill in the blanks with the wish closing from the list that makes the best ending for each paragraph.

1. At last, the school day was over. It had been the worst day ever. To begin with, Robbie had forgotten his homework, so he got in trouble. Then he got a bad grade on his science test and knew his parents would be angry with him. To make things worse, Robbie had a fight with his best friend.

   _____

2. Basically, no one could make a decision about the activities for the party. The girls wanted to have music and dance, but the boys wanted to play games. The holiday party was in two days and nothing was planned.

   _____

3. In other words, I thought a day at the zoo would be boring. Boy, was I wrong! Everyone was shocked to hear that a poisonous snake had escaped from its cage. Just as it was getting exciting, everyone was asked to leave.

   _____

Independently Write your own wish closing for one of the paragraphs above. Use the list of wish words and phrases for help.

_____

Close a Story with a Wish

A writer can choose to end a story with a wish so the character can look forward to something meaningful. A wish at the closing of a story has the reader looking forward to a happy ending.

Wish Words and Phrases

my dream	I wish	hopefully	I want	in my daydreams
I hope I get	if only I	I am hopeful	imagine	look forward to
wish for	I hope	my desire	I intend	with any luck

Whole Group We will write an ending that has a wish.

A. Let's read the ending paragraph. It is missing a closing sentence.

> *In closing, the airplane landed safely, and I survived my first flight. Looking back, I can't believe how frightened I had been. I thought the plane was going to crash. I was so scared before the flight, I even told my parents that I wouldn't go on the vacation.*

Work together to create a list of wish sentences that could be used to end the paragraph above.

1. _____

2. _____

3. _____

B. Which sentence makes the best ending? Vote for your favorite closing sentence.

The winning sentence is number _____ !

Time to Practice!

C. Have you ever done something that you didn't think you could do? Together, write a closing paragraph about something that you thought was too hard to do. First, let's make a list of events to include in the closing paragraph.

1. _____   3. _____

2. _____   4. _____

D. Next, let's write a wish closing that would make sense with the events you listed.

_____

E. Now, on a separate piece of paper, we will write the closing paragraph. Use the events you listed and the winning wish closing. Start the paragraph with an ending transitional word or phrase, such as *finally*, *at last*, *in conclusion*, or *in the end*.

Check Your Work

Does the ending sentence make a wish for the future?

Close a Story with a Wish

A writer can choose to end a story with a wish so the character can look forward to something special or meaningful. Wishes are fun to make, but they don't always come true unless they are magical.

Partners A mystical wizard has just granted you three wishes. With your partner, think of what you would wish for. Then write down the three wishes.

Wish 1: _____

Wish 2: _____

Wish 3: _____

Which of the wishes do you think would be the best one? Why? _____

_____

Independently The wizard is back! This time he is giving you a choice of wishes, but you can only pick one.

> ### Possible Wishes
> To become the smartest person of all time
> To help the world be a better place
> To become a very famous performer
> To become the best athlete in the country
> To be the best-looking person in the world

Which wish would you select? Why do you think that is the best wish for you? How would it change your life or the world? Would you be able to help others or just yourself? Would you become a happier person or do you think it would cause problems? Write about your choice.

I chose to _____ .

I think this is the best wish for me because _____

_____

_____

_____

_____

Whole Group Share your wish with the class.

Close a Story with a Wish

A writer can choose to end a story with a wish so the character can look forward to something meaningful. A wish at the closing of a story has the reader looking forward to a happy ending.

Wish Words and Phrases

my dream	I wish	hopefully	I want	in my daydreams
I hope I get	if only I	I am hopeful	imagine	look forward to
wish for	I hope	my desire	I intend	with any luck

Independently Write an ending with a wish.

A. Fill in each blank with a wish word or phrase from the above list. One of these sentences will be used as a wish closing.

1. _____ that things will be different tomorrow.

2. I _____ buying my new racing bike.

3. _____ is to get better grades in math.

4. I will _____ myself as a star.

B. Select one of the above wish closings for a paragraph. Which wish closing would make the best ending?

The wish closing that would make the best ending is number _____ because
_____.

C. Now make a list of events to include in the paragraph.

1. _____   3. _____

2. _____   4. _____

D. Write an ending paragraph with the wish closing that you selected. Use the events you listed to complete the paragraph. Remember to begin your closing paragraph with a transitional word or phrase, such as *finally*, *at last*, *in conclusion*, or *in the end*.

_____

_____

_____

_____

Check Your Work

Is the closing a happy one?

Whole Group Share your wish with the class.

Close a Story with a Wish

A writer can choose to end a story with a wish so the character can look forward to something meaningful. A wish at the closing of a story has the reader looking forward to a happy ending.

Wish Words and Phrases

my dream	I wish	hopefully	I want	in my daydreams
I hope I get	if only I	I am hopeful	imagine	look forward to
wish for	I hope	my desire	I intend	with any luck

Wish Closings

Someday, I wish I could have a pet.
I intend to get all As on my next report card.
With any luck, my class will win Field Day.
My goal is to be a better friend.

Independently Write a closing paragraph that ends with a wish.

A. Write the wish closing for your paragraph. You may use any of the wish closings above or write your own wish closing using the list of wish sentences.

_____

B. Now make a list of events to include in the paragraph.

1. _____   3. _____

2. _____   4. _____

C. Write an ending paragraph with the wish closing you chose and the events you listed. The closing should be a wish that a character would make for the future. Remember to begin your closing paragraph with a transitional word or phrase, such as *finally*, *at last*, *in conclusion*, or *in the end*.

_____

_____

_____

_____

Check Your Work

Does your wish have the reader looking forward to a happy ending for the character?

Did you begin your closing paragraph with a transition?

Whole Group Share your wish with the class.

Close a Story with a Feeling

I feel so emotional today. First, I was happy, then I was sad, and now I just feel confused. Some days are like that. Your feelings can change very quickly. When you express happiness, sadness, or confusion you are showing your feelings. A writer can use feeling words at the end of a story in order to reveal the character's final emotions.

Example: *The children were laughing and cheering as the clown performed his juggling act. Everyone was having a wonderful time. The clown was delighted to see so many smiling faces. He was thrilled to make so many people happy.*

Feeling Words

curious	confused	brave	excited	scared
angry	proud	afraid	furious	happy
sad	delighted	guilty	impatient	nervous

Feeling Closings

She was sad but knew that next time would be different.

I am curious to find out what I will learn tomorrow.

She realized that she was very impatient with her.

Whole Group Let's give these closing paragraphs an ending that is a feeling. Fill in the blanks with the feeling closing from the list that makes the best closing for each paragraph.

1. Finally, I thought learning about birds would be boring, but I found out that I was wrong. Birds are amazing creatures. They know when to migrate without using a calendar. They know how to build a nest with no instructions. Birds also have different songs for different things. _____

   _____

2. The movie was over, but Christie was still upset. The movie showed children being bullied by a classmate. It reminded her of the time she saw someone being bullied and she did not try to stop it. _____

   _____

3. Thinking back, Beverly knew her little sister, Teri, was only trying to help her. She didn't mean to spill the paint all over her science project. Beverly was so angry she could not stop screaming at her. Finally, Teri cried and ran to her room. _____

   _____

Independently Write your own feeling closing for one of the paragraphs above.

_____

Whole Group Share your feeling closing with the class.

Close a Story with a Feeling

When you express happiness, sadness, or confusion, you are showing your feelings. The emotions of the characters are expressed throughout the story. A writer can close a story with a feeling so that the reader understands the emotions of the characters at the end.

Feeling Words

curious	confused	brave	excited	scared
angry	proud	afraid	furious	happy
sad	delighted	guilty	impatient	nervous

Whole Group We will write an ending with a feeling.

A. Let's read the ending paragraph. It is missing a closing sentence.

> *Consequently, the teacher did not tell my parents. He thought I had been punished enough and had learned a lesson. I only wanted to keep my friend from getting into trouble, but now I realize I was making things worse.*

Think of a time when you tried to help a friend, but everything went wrong. We will create a list of feeling sentences that could be used to end the paragraph above.

1. _____

2. _____

3. _____

B. Vote for the sentence that makes the best ending for the paragraph.

The winning sentence is number _____ !

Time to Practice!

C. Think about a time you helped a friend and everything went right. How did you feel? Together, we will write a closing paragraph about a time you were helpful. First, let's make a list of events to include in the closing paragraph.

1. _____   3. _____

2. _____   4. _____

D. Next, let's write a feeling closing that would make sense with the events you listed.

_____

E. Now, on a separate piece of paper, we will write the closing paragraph. Use the events you listed and the feeling closing you wrote. Start the paragraph with an ending transitional word or phrase.

Check Your Work

Does the ending sentence express the character's feelings?

# Close a Story with a Feeling

Poetry is an imaginative way to express feelings in writing. An acrostic poem is created by writing a word vertically down the page. One letter is written on each line. Each line of the poem must begin with that letter and must describe the vertical word.

Example: *So gloomy*
Always crying
Discouraged

Partners With a partner, write acrostic poems using the feeling words below.

H _____

A _____

P _____

P _____

Y _____

Try another one!

B _____

R _____

A _____

V _____

E _____

Independently Now, write your own acrostic poem. Don't forget that the word or phrase on each line of the poem must describe the vertical feeling word.

S _____

C _____

A _____

R _____

E _____

D _____

Check Your Work

Do the lines of your poems describe the feeling words?

Whole Group Share one of your poems with the class. Explain why you wrote what you did.

Close a Story with a Feeling

A writer can close a story with a feeling so that the reader understands how the characters feel about the story's outcome.

Feeling Words

curious	embarrassed	brave	lucky	scared
angry	proud	afraid	furious	happy
sad	shy	guilty	impatient	nervous
delighted	upset	confused	silly	excited

Independently Write an ending that has a feeling.

A. Fill in each blank with a feeling word from the above list. One of these sentences will be used as a feeling closing.

1. Justin felt _____ . He had kicked the winning goal!

2. My father was so _____ with me.

3. Nicole felt _____ when she got the blue ribbon.

4. Andrew was _____ as he approached the dark house.

B. Select one of the above feeling closings for a paragraph. Circle that number.

C. Make a list of events to include in the paragraph. The events should be written in the order they will happen in the paragraph.

1. _____   3. _____

2. _____   4. _____

D. Write an ending paragraph, using the feeling closing you selected and the events you listed. The closing should express the emotions of the character at the end of the story. Remember to begin your closing paragraph with a transitional word or phrase.

_____

_____

_____

_____

Check Your Work

Does the closing express the character's emotions?
Did you begin your closing paragraph with a transition?

Whole Group Share your feeling closing with the class.

 # Close a Story with a Feeling

When you express happiness or sadness you are showing your feelings. A writer can close a story with a feeling so that the reader understands the emotions of the characters at the end of the story.

Feeling Words

curious	embarrassed	brave	lucky	scared
angry	proud	afraid	furious	happy
sad	shy	guilty	impatient	nervous
delighted	upset	confused	silly	excited

Feeling Closings

Devin was very confused by what his friend had done.

Matthew was embarrassed about what had happened at the game.

Dyana felt brave because she had confronted the bully.

Arriving so late to the surprise party made Jason feel ridiculous.

Independently Write a closing paragraph that ends with a feeling.

A. Write the feeling closing for your paragraph. You may use any of the feeling closings above or write your own using the list of feeling words and phrases.

_____

B. Now make a list of events to include in the paragraph. The events should be written in the order they will happen in the paragraph.

1. _____   3. _____

2. _____   4. _____

C. Write an ending paragraph with the feeling closing you chose and the events you listed. Remember to begin your closing paragraph with a transitional word or phrase.

_____

_____

_____

_____

Check Your Work

Does your closing express the character's feelings?

Did you begin your closing paragraph with a transition?

Whole Group Share your feeling closing with the class.

Close a Story with a Question

A writer can use questions in a story to spark the reader's curiosity. A question is a great way to begin or end a story. A question at the end of a story has the reader wondering about the outcome or thinking about what has happened in a new way.

Example: *The bowling party was over. Kate almost did not go because she is a horrible bowler. She was afraid the other children would laugh at her. In the end, Kate was glad she went. Kate discovered she doesn't have to be the best at something to have a good time. Why had she been so worried?*

Question Words

who	what	where	when	will
how	which	why	whose	am
did	do	is	are	have
were	could	would	was	should

Question Closings

Why is she here?   What could it be?

How will he tell his parents? Where did it come from?

Whole Group Let's end these closing paragraphs with a question. Make sure the question ending makes sense with the rest of the paragraph. Use the lists above for help.

1. Frank saw it, but he still didn't believe it. It had fallen out of a tree and bounced like a ball onto the sidewalk. It looked so strange. It was purple and furry, with huge ears. _____

   _____

2. Lunch was over, and it was time to return to class. As I walked into my classroom, I couldn't believe my eyes. I saw my mother standing in the front of the room talking to my teacher. _____

   _____

3. Last year, Bob thought sharing a room with his brother, Ed, was fun. Now, he feels differently. Ed is always playing his music and making a lot of noise. Bob needs some peace and quiet. He wants his own room.

   _____

Independently Write your own question closing for one of the paragraphs above. Use the list of question words to help you.

_____

Whole Group Share your question closing with the class.

Close a Story with a Question

A writer can use questions to spark the reader's curiosity. A question is a great way to begin or end a story.

Question Words

who	what	where	when	will
how	which	why	whose	am
did	do	is	are	have
were	could	would	was	should

Whole Group We will practice using a question to end a story.

A. Let's read the ending paragraph. It is missing a closing sentence.

After what happened, Estelle was worried that her brother would tell on her. He was such a big tattletale. He always told on her even when it wasn't her fault.

Think of what you would do if you thought someone was going to tattle on you. What would you say? What question would you ask yourself? Let's create a list of question sentences that will have the reader wondering what Estelle will do.

1. _____

2. _____

3. _____

B. Think about the closing question sentences. Which one makes the best ending for the paragraph? Vote for the best ending sentence.

The winner is sentence number _____ !

Time to Practice!

C. Now, we will write a closing paragraph about needing money to buy a gift. First, let's make a list of events to include in the closing paragraph.

1. _____   3. _____

2. _____   4. _____

D. Next, we'll write a question closing that would make sense with the events you listed.

_____

E. Now, on a separate sheet of paper, let's write the closing paragraph. Use the events and the question closing above. Start the paragraph with an ending transition.

Check Your Work

Does the ending sentence cause the reader to stop and think?

Close a Story with a Question

News reporters ask questions that will get them the information they need for their news stories. The reporters ask questions that begin with the words *who*, *what*, *when*, *where*, *why*, and *how*. These words are often called "WH" words because they begin with a W or an H, and ask a question.

Partners NEWS FLASH! School will close a week early. News reporters have arrived at the school to find out why the closing date had been changed. Read the answers below. With a partner, think of the questions that could have been asked. Write the questions on the lines below. Begin each question with a "WH" word.

1. **Question:** _____

   Answer: The children were so well behaved we thought they deserved a longer summer.

2. **Question:** _____

   Answer: The principal and the teacher made the decision.

3. **Question:** _____

   Answer: The decision to close school early was made last week.

4. **Question:** _____

   Answer: We were at school when we thought of the idea.

5. **Question:** _____

   Answer: The parents will be delighted to have their children home for an extra week.

6. **Question:** _____

   Answer: The children will have more time to exercise and have fun.

Independently A carnival is coming to your town. Pretend you are a reporter for a local newspaper. What questions will you ask about the carnival? Use the "WH" words in your questions. Write the questions and the answers on a separate sheet of paper.

Example: *Question: How long will the carnival be in town?*

Answer: The carnival will be in town for one week.

> ### Check Your Work
> What question do you think is the most important? Why?

Whole Group Share one of your interview questions and answers with the class.

Close a Story with a Question

A writer uses a question to spark readers' curiosity and to make them question something in the story. A question at the end of a story has readers wondering about the outcome or thinking about what has happened in a new way.

Question Words

who	what	where	when	will
how	which	why	whose	am
did	do	is	are	have
were	could	would	was	should

Independently Write a closing paragraph with a question.

A. Fill in each blank with a question word from the above list.

1. _____ I ever be done?

2. _____ one should I pick?

3. _____ they really going to leave the puppy?

4. _____ else could go wrong?

5. _____ old do I have to be to get some respect?

B. Select one of the above question closings for a paragraph. Which question closing would make the best ending?

The question closing that would make the best ending is number _____ because _____ .

C. Now make a list of events to include in the paragraph. The events should be written in the order they will happen in the paragraph.

1. _____   3. _____

2. _____   4. _____

D. On a separate piece of paper, write an ending paragraph with the question closing you selected. Include the events you listed. Remember to begin your closing paragraph with a transitional word or phrase, such as *finally*, *at last*, *in conclusion*, or *in the end*.

Check Your Work

Does the closing ask a question related to the story?
Did you begin your closing paragraph with a transition?

Whole Group Share your closing question with the class.

Close a Story with a Question

A writer can use a question to spark readers' curiosity and to make them question something in the story. A question is a great way to begin or end a story. A question at the end of a story has readers wondering about the outcome or thinking about what has happened in a new way.

Question Words

who	what	where	when	will
how	which	why	whose	am
did	do	is	are	have
were	could	would	was	should

Question Closings

What should I do with all this money?
Was it the right thing to do?
Will I become famous someday?

Independently Write a closing paragraph, ending it with a question. You may use any of the question closings above or write your own using the list of question words.

A. Write the question closing for your paragraph.

_____

B. Now make a list of events to include in the paragraph. The events should be written in the order they will happen in the paragraph.

1. _____   3. _____

2. _____   4. _____

C. Write an ending paragraph with the question closing you wrote and the events you listed. The closing should have the character wondering about something at the end of the story. Remember to begin your closing paragraph with a transitional word or phrase, such as *finally*, *at last*, *in conclusion*, or *in the end*.

_____

_____

_____

_____

Check Your Work
Does the ending have a question?
Did you begin your closing paragraph with a transition?

Whole Group Share your closing question with the class.

Describe Appearances

Big, *small*, *young*, *old*, *mighty*, and *weak* are physical adjectives. These adjectives describe appearance. They can describe a person, an animal, or an object. A writer can use physical adjectives to describe a character, so the reader can visualize what the character looks like. The writer creates a character that is vivid and realistic when physical adjectives are used in the story.

Example: *The **huge, powerful** giant stared down at the **small, frail** boy. The boy's **thin** legs were shaking with fear.*

		Physical Adjectives			
plump	awkward	short	tiny	bony	clumsy
fat	young	old	strong	mighty	graceful
dainty	athletic	tall	weak	powerful	thin
huge	skinny	fierce	sickly	frail	feeble

Whole Group We will add physical adjectives to writing.

A. Let's add physical adjectives to the following sentences. The adjectives must describe the physical appearance of the characters. Use the list above for help.

1. The _____ , _____ boy won the race.

2. A _____ lion chased the _____ zebra.

3. A _____ actress was spotted by the large crowd.

B. Let's list physical adjectives that could describe the following nouns. Use the words in the box for help. Choose physical adjectives that have not been used.

1. **tree:** _____ 3. **doctor:** _____

2. **troll:** _____ 4. **rabbit:** _____

C. We will use the physical adjectives that describe a rabbit to write a sentence. The sentence should help the reader visualize the rabbit's appearance.

_____

_____

Independently Independently, write descriptive sentences about the other nouns in Part B. Choose two or more physical adjectives to describe each noun.

1. _____

2. _____

3. _____

Whole Group Share your favorite sentence with the class.

Describe Appearances

A writer can use physical adjectives to describe a character so the reader can visualize the character's appearance. The character could be a person, an animal, or an object.

Physical Adjectives

plump	awkward	short	tiny	bony	clumsy
fat	young	old	strong	mighty	graceful
dainty	athletic	tall	weak	powerful	thin
huge	skinny	fierce	sickly	frail	feeble

Whole Group We will write a descriptive paragraph using physical adjectives to describe a baseball player. The physical adjectives should help the reader visualize the baseball player's appearance.

Brainstorming Time!

A. First, we will write physical adjectives that could describe the baseball player. Use the words from the list or any other physical adjectives.

1. _____   3. _____

2. _____   4. _____

B. Now, let's fill in the information below about the baseball player. We will include this information in the descriptive paragraph about the baseball player.

1. **Age and Height:** _____

2. **Description of Hair and Eyes:** _____

C. Let's create some great Super Starter opening sentences that could start our paragraph.

1. _____

2. _____

3. _____

D. Vote for your favorite opening sentence.

The winning opening sentence is number _____ !

E. Now, we will continue writing to complete the descriptive paragraph on a separate sheet of paper. Use the winning sentence and the information above.

Check Your Work

After reading the paragraph, can you visualize the baseball player?

Describe Appearances

Adjectives can be used to describe a character's appearance. A writer can use physical adjectives to describe a character so the reader can visualize what the character looks like.

Partners   In pairs, practice using physical adjectives.

A. Find and circle the physical adjectives in the word search below. The physical adjectives are written horizontally, vertically, diagonally, or from bottom to top.

```
W  W  C  A  T  E  C  X  I  R
Y  S  M  U  L  C  I  D  X  U
P  U  K  H  N  R  T  D  S  R
M  O  U  I  K  E  N  M  M  V
R  G  W  D  D  I  A  T  A  F
E  O  F  E  U  F  G  Z  L  Q
B  E  H  O  R  R  I  B  L  E
J  C  J  U  M  F  G  Z  X  G
G  U  P  S  D  Y  U  U  K  K
S  T  R  O  N  G  J  L  I  R
```

Word Box

fat	gigantic
strong	horrible
huge	powerful
clumsy	hideous
small	fierce

B. Read the paragraph. With your partner, fill in the blanks with the physical adjectives from Part A.

Nicholas ran and ran until he couldn't run anymore. At last, he spied a (1) _____ tree and hid behind it. Nicholas looked down the street, but he could not see any signs of the (2) _____ , (3) _____ monster that had been chasing after him. The monster was (4) _____ with (5) _____ arms and legs. Its (6) _____ , (7) _____ eyes had glared at Nicholas and made him shake with fear. However, the monster was (8) _____ and (9) _____ , so he could not run fast. Nicholas was able to race away from this (10) _____ creature. Nicholas knew he would never forget how lucky he had been to escape.

C. Write another paragraph on a separate piece of paper. Instead of a monster following someone, this time, it is a baby. Include any physical adjectives of your choice.

Check Your Work

Do the physical adjectives clearly describe the baby?

Whole Group Share a descriptive sentence from your paragraph with the class.

73

Describe Appearances

A writer can use physical adjectives to describe a character so the reader can visualize the character's appearance. Writers can use physical adjectives throughout their stories to describe any person or thing.

Independently Use physical adjectives to write a story ending.

A. Read the following physical adjectives.

lively   young   strong

A noun is a word that names a person, place, thing, or idea. What nouns can be described using the three physical adjectives above? Write the nouns.

_____

B. Select one of the above nouns to use as the main character in a descriptive paragraph. Which noun did you select?

The noun I chose is _____ because _____

_____ .

C. Begin the descriptive paragraph with a Super Starter opening sentence. Write two Super Starters. Choose the one you like best for the opening sentence.

1. _____

2. _____

D. Now make a list of events to include in the paragraph. The events should be written in the order they will happen in the paragraph.

1. _____   3. _____

2. _____   4. _____

E. Write a descriptive paragraph with the information from Parts A–D. The physical adjectives should paint a vivid picture of the main character. Physical adjectives should also be used to describe any nouns or pronouns in the paragraph to help the reader understand and visualize what is happening.

_____

_____

_____

_____

Check Your Work
Does the descriptive paragraph paint a vivid picture?

Whole Group Share a descriptive sentence from your paragraph with the class.

Describe Appearances

A writer can use physical adjectives to describe a character so the reader can visualize what the character looks like. The writer creates a character that is vivid and realistic when physical adjectives are used in the story.

Physical Adjectives

plump	awkward	short	tiny	bony	clumsy
fat	young	old	strong	mighty	graceful
dainty	athletic	tall	weak	powerful	thin
huge	skinny	fierce	sickly	frail	feeble

List of Characters

a talking teddy bear   a robot   your favorite actor

Independently Write a descriptive paragraph.

A. Think of a main character for the paragraph and three or more physical adjectives to describe the character. Use the box for ideas. Write them down here.

Character: _____

Physical Adjectives: _____

B. Write a Super Starter that could start the paragraph.

_____

C. Now make a list of events to include in the paragraph. The events should be written in the order they will happen in the paragraph.

1. _____   3. _____

2. _____   4. _____

D. Write a descriptive paragraph with the information from Parts A–C. The physical adjectives should describe the characters and other nouns in the paragraph.

_____

_____

_____

_____

Check Your Work

Does the descriptive paragraph paint a vivid picture?

Whole Group Share a descriptive sentence from your paragraph with the class.

Whole Group/Independently

Day 1
Electrifying Elaborations

Describe Details

When people describe how things sound, look, taste, feel, and smell, they use adjectives. Writers often describe nouns by using the five senses. Using sensory adjectives will engage the reader and make the story easier to understand.

Example: *The screaming boy refused to leave the kitchen without a delicious, warm cookie. Suddenly, his mom appeared with a big glass of cold milk and a shiny plate full of tasty cookies.*

Sensory Adjectives

Sight	Sound	Taste	Touch	Smell
colorful	noisy	salty	damp	pleasant
bright	whispery	spicy	soft	sweet
dull	booming	delicious	rough	foul
shiny	screechy	sour	cold	sweaty
sparkling	moaning	bitter	fluffy	fresh

Whole Group We will use sensory adjectives in sentences.

A. Let's add sensory adjectives to the following sentences. The sensory adjectives must describe a person, place, or thing. Use the list above for help.

1. The team celebrated by enjoying a _____ , _____ pizza.

2. What a _____ , _____ sound the thunder made!

3. Nicole thought her brother smelled _____ after his football game.

4. Jonathan loved to sleep on his _____ , _____ pillow.

B. Let's list sensory adjectives that could describe the following nouns. Use any sensory adjectives of your choice or find words from the list above.

1. **apple:** _____   3. **firecracker:** _____

2. **snow:** _____   4. **restaurant:** _____

C. Let's use the sensory adjectives that describe a restaurant to write a sentence. The sentence should help the reader create a mental picture of the restaurant.

_____

Independently Independently, write sentences about the other nouns in Part B.

1. _____

2. _____

3. _____

Whole Group Share your favorite sentence with the class.

Describe Details

Writers often describe nouns by using the five senses. A writer can use sensory adjectives to create a mental picture of the characters, places, and things in a story.

Sensory Adjectives

Sight	Sound	Taste	Touch	Smell
colorful	noisy	salty	damp	pleasant
bright	whisper	spicy	soft	sweet
dull	booming	delicious	rough	foul
shiny	screech	sour	cold	sweaty
sparkling	moaning	bitter	fluffy	fresh

Whole Group As a group, we will write a paragraph describing a day at the beach.

Brainstorming Time!

A. Think about the following questions and write what characters, places, and things could be found at the beach. Let's write one answer for each question. Then we'll write one or more sensory adjectives to describe it.

	Answers	**Sensory Adjectives**
1. What could you see?	_____	_____
2. What could you hear?	_____	_____
3. What could you taste?	_____	_____
4. What could you feel?	_____	_____
5. What could you smell?	_____	_____

B. Now let's write a Super Starter opening sentence for our paragraph.

_____

C. Next, we'll make a list of events to include in the paragraph.

1. _____   3. _____

2. _____   4. _____

D. It is time for us to write the paragraph about a day at the beach on a separate sheet of paper. Begin with the winning Super Starter opening. Then include the information from Parts A and C to complete the paragraph. Create a clear picture in the reader's mind by using sensory adjectives.

Check Your Work

Did the sensory adjectives help you to imagine a day at the beach?

Describe Details

Writers often describe nouns by using the five senses. Sensory adjectives give the reader clues about the characters, places, and things in a story.

Partners   Sensory adjectives can be used as clues to solve a riddle. In pairs, solve the riddle below and then write one of your own.

A. In the riddle below, each clue will give you more information about the answer. Write a guess for what you think the answer is after each clue. Follow the clues in order.

Clues	Guesses
1. It is a place.	_____
2. You can hear loud, cheerful music.	_____
3. You can smell animals.	_____
4. You can touch the metal seat.	_____
5. You can taste cotton candy.	_____
6. You can see big colorful tents.	_____
7. What place is this?	

B. Reread the riddle. Do all the clues make sense with your final answer?

C. Now write a riddle using sensory clues. The riddle will be about another place. You can have classmates guess the riddle when you are finished.

Clues	Guesses
1. It is a place.	_____
2. You can hear _____ .	_____
3. You can smell _____ .	_____
4. You can touch _____ .	_____
5. You can taste _____ .	_____
6. You can see _____ .	_____
7. What place is this?	

Independently On a separate piece of paper, write a riddle using sensory clues. The riddle can be about any place. Include clues that create a vivid image. You can have classmates guess the riddle when you are finished.

Whole Group Volunteer to share one of your riddles with the class.

Describe Details

Writers often describe nouns by using the five senses. When people describe how things *sound*, *look*, *taste*, *feel*, and *smell*, they use sensory adjectives. A writer can use sensory adjectives to create a mental picture of the characters, places, and things in a story. Using sensory adjectives will engage the reader and make the story easier to understand.

Independently Write a paragraph, creating a mental picture with sensory adjectives.

A. Read the following sensory adjectives. Can you think of something each of these sensory adjectives could describe? Could it be a place? Could it be a character? Could it be a thing? Write down a noun each of these sensory adjectives could describe.

1. **bright:** _____

2. **damp:** _____

3. **noisy:** _____

4. **sour:** _____

B. Select one of the sensory adjectives and the noun it describes from the list above to use as the main idea in a paragraph. Circle that number.

C. Begin the paragraph with a Super Starter opening sentence.

_____

D. Now make a list of events to include in the paragraph. The events should be written in the order they will happen in the paragraph.

1. _____

2. _____

3. _____

E. Write a paragraph with the information from Parts A–D. The sensory adjectives in the paragraph should create a mental picture of the characters, places, and things in the story. Use sensory adjectives to create vivid images throughout the paragraph.

_____

_____

_____

_____

```
Check Your Work
Do the sensory adjectives create a mental picture for the reader?
```

Whole Group Choose a sentence from your paragraph that includes sensory adjectives. Share your sentence with the class.

Describe Details

Writers often describe nouns by using the five senses. A writer can use sensory adjectives to create a mental picture of the characters, places, and things in a story.

Independently Write a paragraph using sensory adjectives.

Sensory Adjectives

Sight	Sound	Taste	Touch	Smell
colorful	noisy	salty	damp	pleasant
bright	whisper	spicy	soft	sweet
dull	booming	delicious	rough	foul
shiny	screech	sour	cold	sweaty
sparkling	moaning	bitter	fluffy	fresh

Story Ideas

Being the first one at a party.   Missing the bus.
Playing on a basketball team.   Going roller skating.

A. Choose a topic from the box, or think of one of your own. Now, read the following questions. Only answer the questions that make sense with your topic.

1. **What could you hear?** _____

2. **What could you see?** _____

3. **What could you taste?** _____

4. **What could you touch?** _____

5. **What could you smell?** _____

B. Write a Super Starter opening sentence that could begin the paragraph.

_____

C. Now make a list of events to include in the paragraph. The events should be written in the order they will happen in the paragraph.

1. _____   3. _____

2. _____   4. _____

D. On a separate piece of paper, write a paragraph with the information from Parts A–C. The sensory adjectives should create a mental picture for the reader.

Check Your Work

Do the sensory adjectives help the reader understand the paragraph?

Whole Group Choose a sentence from your paragraph that includes sensory adjectives. Share your sentence with the class.

Describe Emotions

How are you feeling? Are you happy, sad, afraid, or worried? These words express your emotions. Writers bring the feelings and thoughts of characters to life by using adjectives. Writers use emotion adjectives to help the reader connect to the feelings of the characters.

Example: *The students were excited as they lined up for their class picture. Everyone was talking. Frustrated, the photographer walked away from the camera to wait for everyone to be quiet.*

Emotion Adjectives

miserable	upset	grumpy	excited	sympathetic
ecstatic	surprised	anxious	worried	jealous
annoyed	bored	frustrated	confident	irritated
frightened	cheerful	lonely	discouraged	enthusiastic

Whole Group As a group, we will practice thinking about emotion adjectives.

A. Let's add emotion adjectives to the following sentences. The words must express the feelings of the characters. Use the emotion adjectives from the above list for help.

1. The girl felt _____ after dropping her new cell phone.

2. I was so _____ when I heard about the poster contest.

3. Osvaldo was very _____ while sitting in class waiting for the teacher to hand back the math tests.

B. Here are some emotion adjectives. What could make a character feel each emotion?

Example: *happy: a birthday party*

1. **enthusiastic:** _____   3. **frightened:** _____

2. **miserable:** _____   4. **surprised:** _____

C. Let's use the emotion adjective *surprised* with the idea from Part B to write a sentence about a character that is surprised by or about something.

_____

Independently Now it is your turn to write sentences with the remaining emotion adjectives. Use the ideas from Part B to write the sentences. The sentences must express the emotions of each character.

1. _____

2. _____

3. _____

Whole Group Share your favorite sentence with the class.

Describe Emotions

Writers can bring the feelings and thoughts of characters to life by using adjectives. A writer can use emotion adjectives to help the reader connect to the feelings of the characters.

Emotion Adjectives

miserable	upset	grumpy	excited	sympathetic
ecstatic	surprised	anxious	worried	jealous
annoyed	bored	frustrated	confident	irritated
frightened	cheerful	lonely	discouraged	enthusiastic

Whole Group Let's write a paragraph using emotion adjectives. The paragraph will be about an actor in a school play who forgot his lines. Think about how the actor would feel.

Brainstorming Time!

A. First, we will write emotion adjectives that could describe the actor's feelings. Use the emotion adjectives from the list or any other emotion adjective.

1. _____   3. _____

2. _____   4. _____

B. The paragraph should begin with a Super Starter opening sentence. Think of some great Super Starter openings for our paragraph.

1. _____

2. _____

Vote for your favorite opening sentence.

The winning opening sentence is number _____ !

C. Next, we'll make a list of events to include in the paragraph. The events should be written in the order they will appear in the story.

1. _____   3. _____

2. _____   4. _____

D. It is time for us to write the paragraph about the forgetful actor on a separate piece of paper. Begin with the winning Super Starter opening and include the events you listed. Describe the actor's feelings throughout the paragraph by including the emotion adjectives from Part A.

Check Your Work

After reading the paragraph, do you understand how the actor felt?

Describe Emotions

Adjectives can express feelings. Writers bring the thoughts and emotions of characters to life by using adjectives. A writer can use emotion adjectives to help the reader connect to the feelings of the characters.

Partners Explore synonyms and emotion adjectives in the following activities.

A. With a partner, read the clues for the crossword puzzle. The clues are synonyms for the emotion adjectives in the word box. They have the same or nearly the same meanings. Find the synonym for each clue and complete the crossword puzzle.

Emotion Crossword Puzzle

Across
2. scared
3. confused
5. grouchy
7. sad
8. uninterested
9. worried
10. envious

Down
1. happy
4. thrilled
6. annoyed

Word Box

miserable	weary
grumpy	lonely
excited	puzzled
anxious	jealous
upset	cheerful
joyful	irritated
confident	bored
frightened	

B. With your partner, write a paragraph about getting a bad haircut. Include as many of the emotion adjectives from the crossword puzzle as you can to express how the character is feeling about the haircut.

_____

_____

_____

_____

┌───┐
Check Your Work
Do the adjectives clearly express the feelings of the character?
└───┘

Whole Group Share your paragraph with the class.

Describe Emotions

A writer can use adjectives to express the thoughts and emotions of characters in a story. Writers use emotion adjectives to help the reader relate to the feelings of the characters. Emotion adjectives can bring the characters to life.

Independently Describe emotions in a paragraph.

A. Read the following emotion adjectives.

surprised   **ecstatic**   **confident**

Can you think of a time when you felt all of the above emotions? Was it a contest you won or did you make a new friend? Write down situations when someone could experience these emotions.

1. _____

2. _____

3. _____

B. Select one of the above situations to use as the main idea in a paragraph.

C. Think of a Super Starter opening sentence to begin your paragraph.

_____

D. Now make a list of events to include in the paragraph. The events should be written in the order they will happen in the paragraph.

1. _____   3. _____

2. _____   4. _____

E. Write a paragraph with the information from Parts A–D. The emotion adjectives in the paragraph should express the feelings of the main character. Use emotion adjectives to make the characters believable.

_____

_____

_____

_____

_____

Check Your Work

Does the paragraph express the emotions of the main character?

Whole Group Choose a sentence from your paragraph that includes adjectives that describe your character's emotions. Share your sentence with the class.

Describe Emotions

A writer can use adjectives to express the feelings of the characters. When characters are believable and show real emotions, the story will come to life.

Independently Write a paragraph using emotion adjectives. You may write about any of the story ideas below or think of your own.

Emotion Adjectives

miserable	upset	grumpy	excited	sympathetic
ecstatic	surprised	anxious	worried	jealous
annoyed	bored	frustrated	confident	irritated
frightened	cheerful	lonely	discouraged	enthusiastic

Story Ideas

Having a sleepover   Losing your homework
Going to the dentist   Finding a squirrel in the house

A. Choose a main character for your paragraph and three or more emotion adjectives to describe the character's feelings.

Character: _____

Emotion Adjectives: _____

B. Write a Super Starter opening sentence for your paragraph.

_____

C. Now make a list of events to include in the paragraph.

1. _____   3. _____

2. _____   4. _____

D. Write a paragraph with the information from Parts A–C. The emotion adjectives should describe the main character's feelings. Emotion adjectives should also be used to describe the feelings of any character in the paragraph.

_____

_____

_____

Check Your Work

Does the paragraph connect the reader with the main character?

Whole Group Choose a sentence from your paragraph that includes adjectives that describe your character's emotions. Share your sentence with the class.

Describe Character Traits

Fantastic, selfish, talented, and *impatient* are adjectives that describe personal characteristics. A writer can show a character's personality by describing his or her character traits.

Example: *The **thoughtful** daughter surprised her mother by planting a flower garden. She **skillfully** arranged the plants in a beautiful pattern. Her mother was shocked when she saw what her **ambitious** daughter had done.*

Personal Characteristic Adjectives

shy	clever	stubborn	thoughtful	humorous
conceited	selfish	generous	motivated	rude
adventurous	impolite	lazy	successful	respectful
affectionate	ambitious	creative	impatient	forgiving

Whole Group As a group, we will practice using personal characteristic adjectives.

A. Let's add personal characteristic adjectives to the following sentences. The words must describe the character's personality. Use the list above for help.

1. Drew was _____ and could hardly wait for his turn at bat.

2. Vicky's puppy was so _____ , it would not stop licking her face.

3. My _____ sister would not share her candy with me.

B. Let's match the characters in column A with the personal characteristics in column B. Write the letter from column B before each sentence in column A.

Column A	**Column B**
1. _____ A parent giving good advice	A. stubborn
2. _____ A clown making people laugh	B. wise
3. _____ A mother hugging her baby	C. adventurous
4. _____ A child that won't stop playing	D. humorous
5. _____ An astronaut going into space	E. affectionate

C. Let's write a sentence using that personal characteristic word to describe the parent who is giving the good advice.

_____

Independently Now it is your turn to write a sentence using one of the characters from Part B. The sentence should describe each character's negative or positive personality traits.

_____

Whole Group Share your sentence with the class.

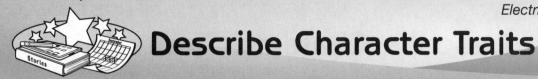

Describe Character Traits

Personal characteristic words are adjectives that describe a character's personality. A writer can help the reader understand a character's personality by showing the negative and positive traits of the character.

Personal Characteristic Adjectives

shy	clever	stubborn	thoughtful	humorous
conceited	selfish	generous	motivated	rude
adventurous	impolite	lazy	successful	respectful
affectionate	ambitious	creative	impatient	forgiving

Whole Group As a group, we will write a paragraph using personal characteristic words. The paragraph will be about a character doing something new and different. What kind of person would do something he or she has never done before?

Brainstorming Time!

A. First, let's write personal characteristic words that could describe the personality of the character. Use words from the list or any other personal characteristic adjectives.

1. _____   3. _____

2. _____   4. _____

B. Now, we'll think of some great Super Starter openings for our paragraph.

1. _____

2. _____

3. _____

Vote for your favorite opening sentence.

The winning opening sentence is number _____ !

C. Next, let's make a list of events to include in the paragraph.

1. _____   3. _____

2. _____   4. _____

D. It is time for us to write, on a separate piece of paper, a paragraph about someone doing something different. Begin with the winning Super Starter opening from Part B and include the events from Part C. Describe the character's personality throughout the paragraph by including the personal characteristic words from Part A.

Check Your Work

Did you use negative or positive personal characteristic words?

Describe Character Traits

Personal characteristic words are adjectives that describe a character's personality. A writer can help the reader understand a character's personality by showing the negative and positive traits of the character.

Partners   With your partner, use personal characteristic adjectives to describe characters.

A. Read the clues. Then unscramble the letters to find the answer. The answer will be a personal characteristic adjective from the word box.

Word Box

impolite	wise	humorous	creative	impatient
successful	rude	conceited	clever	generous
motivated	lazy	stubborn	selfish	shy

Definition	Scrambled Word	Answer
1. overly proud of one's self	eiccndeto	_____
2. gives and shares	ngeesuro	_____
3. funny	hsoouumr	_____
4. only caring for one's self	sheflsi	_____
5. unable to wait	ittpaimen	_____
6. not polite	duer	_____

B. Fill in the blanks using the answers above and other personal characteristic words.

"Give that back!" screamed Paul. Paul was very _____ . He never shared. He would grab things away from children and yell at them. Paul was so _____ that he pushed and shoved without saying, "Excuse me." Paul could never wait his turn. He was very _____ with everyone. The worst part about Paul was that he thought he was the best at everything. He was _____ .

Julia was the opposite of her brother, Paul. Julia was always _____ with what she had. All Julia's friends thought she was a _____ girl. Julia told funny jokes and made everyone laugh. She was very _____ . Julia was never _____ . All Julia's friends thought that she was _____ because she could make up the best games. Being so clever, maybe Julia could teach her brother some manners.

Check Your Work

Do the adjectives describe both characters' personalities?

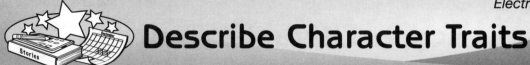

Describe Character Traits

Some adjectives can describe a character's personality. A writer can help the reader understand a character's personality by showing his or her negative and positive traits. The character's actions are explained by using personal characteristic adjectives in the story.

Independently Use personal characteristic adjectives in a paragraph.

A. Read the following personal characteristic adjectives.

affectionate   **forgiving**   **clever**

Can you think of a situation when your parent or guardian would show the personal characteristics above? Would it be a time you did something wrong? Would it be on a special day? Write down situations when your parent or guardian could demonstrate these personal characteristics.

1. _____

2. _____

3. _____

B. Select one of the above situations to use as the main idea in a paragraph.

C. Write a Super Starter opening sentence for your paragraph.

_____

D. Now make a list of events to include in the paragraph. The events should be written in the order they will happen in the paragraph.

1. _____   3. _____

2. _____   4. _____

E. Write a paragraph with the information from Parts A–D. The personal characteristic words in the paragraph should express the negative or positive traits of any character in the story.

_____

_____

_____

_____

Check Your Work

Do the adjectives help the reader understand the characters' behavior?

Whole Group Volunteer to share your paragraph with the class.

Describe Character Traits

Some adjectives can describe a character's personality. A writer can help the reader understand a character's personality by showing the negative and positive traits of the character.

Independently Write a paragraph using personal characteristic words. You may write about any of the characters below or think of your own.

Personal Characteristic Adjectives

shy	clever	stubborn	thoughtful	humorous
conceited	selfish	generous	motivated	rude
adventurous	impolite	lazy	successful	respectful
affectionate	ambitious	creative	impatient	forgiving

Characters

A waitress   The President   A witch   A grandparent   A magician

---

A. Below, write the main character for the paragraph and three or more personal characteristic adjectives to describe the character's personality.

Character: _____

Adjectives: _____

B. Write a Super Starter opening sentence for your paragraph.

_____

C. Now make a list of events to include in the paragraph.

1. _____   3. _____

2. _____   4. _____

D. Write a paragraph with the information from Parts A–C. The personal characteristic adjectives should describe the negative and positive traits of the character and any other character in the paragraph.

_____

_____

_____

_____

Check Your Work

Is the personality of the character clearly described?

Whole Group Choose a sentence from your paragraph that includes adjectives that describe your character's personality. Share your sentence with the class.

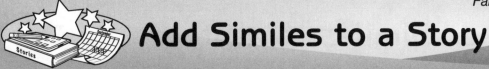

Add Similes to a Story

As quick as a bunny, we will learn about similes. *As quick as a bunny* is a simile. It means to go very fast. A simile is a type of figurative language. Similes are used to say how one thing is similar to a different thing. The things are compared in the sentence by using the words *as* or *like*.

For example, in the simile *as quick as a bunny, we will learn about similes*, a bunny's speed is being compared to the pace at which we will learn about similes—quickly!

> **Example:** *Sandy and Helen were best friends. They liked to do the same things and did everything together. The girls were like two peas in a pod.*

The simile *two peas in a pod* means that the girls were very similar. They are compared to peas in a pod because peas in a pod all look very similar and grow close together. The comparison is made by including the word "like" in the sentence. Writers use similes to make the descriptions of things more vivid or powerful.

Similes

as blind as a bat	*Think: Do bats navigate by sight?*
like a dream	*Think: Can dreams be better than real life?*
as light as a feather	*Think: How heavy is a feather?*
swim like a fish	*Think: How well can fish swim?*

Whole Group Let's complete the following sentences with the similes from the above list. You may change the tense of the verb to make the sentence correct. The simile should show how two different things are similar. Circle the two things that are being compared in each sentence.

1. Our vacation was _____ because it was so perfect.

2. Chrissy _____ and won the competition.

3. Without her glasses, Mary Ann was _____ .

4. Brandon's backpack was _____ on his last day of school.

Independently Write sentences of your own using similes from the above list. Circle the two things that are being compared in each sentence.

1. _____

   _____

2. _____

   _____

Whole Group Share your favorite sentence with the class.

Add Similes to a Story

A simile is a phrase that expresses how one thing is similar to a different thing. The things are compared in the sentence by using the words *as* or *like*. A writer can use similes to make the descriptions of things more vivid or powerful.

Similes

as slow as a snail	*Think: How slowly do snails move?*
fight like cats and dogs	*Think: Do cats and dogs usually get along?*
as stubborn as a mule	*Think: Are mules known for being stubborn?*
as busy as a bee	*Think: Do bees seem very busy?*

Whole Group Let's write a paragraph using similes. The paragraph will be about convincing someone to do something. Do you want someone to go somewhere or to help you with a project?

Brainstorming Time!

A. First, we will write similes that could be used in the paragraph. Use the similes from the list to help you or any other similes that you know.

    1. _____   2. _____

B. Together, we'll think of a great Super Starter opening for the paragraph.

    _____

C. Next, we'll make a list of events to include in the paragraph.

    1. _____   3. _____

    2. _____   4. _____

D. It is time for us to write the paragraph about trying to convince someone to do something. Begin with the Super Starter opening and use the events from Part C to complete the paragraph. Include both similes from Part A to make our descriptions vivid.

_____

_____

_____

_____

Check Your Work

Did the similes make the things you described vivid?

Add Similes to a Story

Similes describe how one thing is like another thing. Similes create vivid and fun images in the mind of the reader.

It is easy to create similes by using the following patterns.

1. verb + "like" + noun **Example:** *swim like a fish*

2. "as" + adjective + "as" + noun **Example:** *as hard as a rock*

Partners With your partner, practice creating and using similes.

A. Fill in each blank with a noun to create a simile. The noun must make sense with the verb or the adjectives.

Verb Simile	**Adjective Simile**
1. runs like _____	5. as strong as _____
2. hops like _____	6. as loud as _____
3. smells like _____	7. as tall as_____
4. screams like _____	8. as red as _____

B. Pick a verb simile and an adjective simile from Part A. Write a complete sentence with each of these similes.

1. _____

2. _____

Independently Write sentences with the other similes from Part A.

1. _____

2. _____

3. _____

4. _____

5. _____

6. _____

Check Your Work

Do the similes make the sentences more vivid and fun?

Whole Group Share one of the sentences with the class.

Add Similes to a Story

A simile is a phrase that expresses how one thing is similar to a different thing. The things are compared in the sentence by using the words *as* or *like*.

Example: *The sun set like an egg yolk breaking open.*

In the example above, the sun is being compared to something unusual. The image is vivid because you can picture bright egg yolk spreading across something. You can make similes by comparing something to something unusual if it creates the right image for the reader.

Similes

as blind as a bat	swim like a fish
as busy as a bee	fight like cats and dogs
like a dream	as light as a feather
as stubborn as a mule	as slow as a snail

Independently Use similes in a paragraph about yourself.

A. Have you ever done something that you didn't think you could do? What was it? How did you feel after you accomplished it? Write down what you did.

I _____ .

B. Write similes that could be included in a paragraph about doing something that you didn't know you could do. Use similes from the list or any similes of your choice.

1. _____   3. _____

2. _____   4. _____

C. Write a Super Starter opening sentence to begin your paragraph.

_____

D. Now make a list of events to include in the paragraph. The events should be written in the order they will happen in the paragraph.

1. _____   3. _____

2. _____   4. _____

E. On a separate piece of paper, write a paragraph with the information from Parts A–D. It is not necessary to include all of the similes from Part B. Only use the similes that best describe things in your paragraph in a vivid or powerful way.

Check Your Work

Do the similes create a vivid mental picture?

Whole Group Choose a sentence from your paragraph that includes a simile you like. Share your sentence with the class.

Add Similes to a Story

One way to create a vivid or powerful mental picture in the reader's mind is by using similes. A simile describes how a thing is similar to a different thing and uses the word *as* or *like*.

Similes

as blind as a bat	swim like a fish
as busy as a bee	fight like cats and dogs
like a dream	as light as a feather
as stubborn as a mule	as slow as a snail

Story Ideas

Meeting your hero	Feeling embarrassed
Learning a new sport	Going to an aquarium

Independently Write a paragraph using similes. Use an idea from the box or think of your own.

A. Write similes that could be included in your paragraph.

1. _____   3. _____

2. _____   4. _____

B. Now write down a Super Starter sentence you can use to begin your paragraph.

_____

C. Make a list of events to include in the paragraph. The events should be written in the order they will happen in the paragraph.

1. _____   3. _____

2. _____   4. _____

D. Write a paragraph with the information from Parts A–C. It is not necessary to include all of the similes from Part A. Only use the similes that describe things in your paragraph in a vivid way.

_____

_____

_____

_____

Check Your Work

Do the similes help the reader to visualize things in the paragraph?

Whole Group Volunteer to share your paragraph with the class.

Add Metaphors to a Story

Metaphors are a breeze to learn, so let's begin. The phrase *metaphors are a breeze* is a metaphor. It means that metaphors are easy to learn, reminding the writer of how a breeze can flow by quickly and easily. A metaphor is a type of figurative language. Metaphors are used to compare two different things. The things are compared in the sentence without using the words *as* or *like*.

> **Example:** *The game was over. Ed knew he had done his best, but his team had still lost. He was very disappointed and was **feeling blue**.*

The metaphor *feeling blue* means sad. Ed's feelings are being compared to the word *blue*, which is often thought of as a sad color. Writers use metaphors to create powerful and lasting images for the reader.

Metaphors

is a baby	*Think:* Do babies behave maturely?
has butter fingers	*Think:* Is butter slippery?
is a rock	*Think:* Are rocks strong and dependable?
smells fishy	*Think:* If something smells fishy, is there something wrong with it?

Whole Group Let's complete the following sentences with the metaphors from the above list. You may change the tense of the verb to make the sentence correct. The metaphor should compare two different things without using the words *like* or *as*. Circle the two things that are being compared in each sentence.

1. Emily _____ when she cries about silly things.

2. David _____ because he kept dropping things.

3. Raul thought the salesman's promises _____ .

4. My teacher _____ ; every day, he's there, ready to help.

Independently Write sentences with metaphors from the above list. Circle the two things that are being compared in each sentence.

1. _____

2. _____

Whole Group Share your favorite sentence with the class.

Add Metaphors to a Story

A metaphor is a type of figurative language. Metaphors are used to describe something by showing how it is like something else. The things are compared in the sentence without using the words *as* or *like*. Writers use metaphors to create powerful images for the reader.

Metaphors

heart of a lion	*Think: Do you think of lions as being brave?*
a couch potato	*Think: What do potatoes do all their lives?*
boiling mad	*Think: Is boiling water cool and peaceful?*
a blanket of snow	*Think: When snow is covering the ground, does it look like a blanket?*

Whole Group Have you ever seen a professional baseball game? Did you watch it on television or were you at the stadium? Was it exciting? Did your favorite team play? We will write a paragraph about watching a professional baseball game.

Brainstorming Time!

A. First, we will write metaphors that could be used in the paragraph. Use the metaphors from the list to help you or use any other metaphors that you know.

1. _____   3. _____

2. _____   4. _____

B. Think of some great Super Starter openings for our paragraph.

1. _____

2. _____

Vote for your favorite opening sentence.

The winning opening sentence is number _____ !

C. Next, we'll make a list of events to include in the paragraph.

1. _____   3. _____

2. _____   4. _____

D. On a separate piece of paper, let's write the paragraph about watching a professional baseball game. We need to include the winning Super Starter opening, the events from Part C, and two metaphors from Part A to create a lasting impression.

Check Your Work

Did the metaphors create a powerful image for the reader?

Add Metaphors to a Story

Metaphors are used to compare two different things that have something in common. Sometimes, writers use one metaphor for an entire paragraph or poem.

Example: *Talent is a boat you build for yourself. You work hard every day, and before you know it, you are sailing off to new possibilities.*

In the above example, an abstract noun (like a quality, feeling, or idea) is being compared to a concrete noun (something you can touch). This metaphor is telling readers that although talent seems wonderful and mysterious, you can develop it yourself through hard work.

Abstract Nouns	
jealousy	confidence
worry	power
curiosity	imagination
intelligence	honesty

Concrete Nouns	
desk	gate
flower	costume
hat	ice cream
candle	cake

Partners In pairs, create a metaphor.

A. With your partner, choose an abstract noun from the first box and a concrete noun from the second. Compare them without using the words *like* or *as*. Feel free to describe the concrete noun with an adjective.

Example: *Imagination is a silly hat.*

_____ is a _____ .

B. Now, list some things the two nouns have in common.

1. _____   3. _____

2. _____   4. _____

C. Now write out the whole paragraph. Write your metaphor sentence from Part A. Then, describe the concrete noun in a way that also makes sense for the abstract noun, using one or more of your comparisons from Part B.

_____

_____

_____

Check Your Work

Did you write the metaphor without using *like* or *as*?

Does the metaphor show a way to think about an abstract noun?

Whole Group Share your metaphor with the class.

Add Metaphors to a Story

Metaphors are used to describe one thing by comparing it to something else. The things are compared in the sentence without using the words *as* or *like*. Writers use metaphors to create powerful and lasting images for the reader.

Metaphors

has butter fingers	is a baby	heart of a lion	a couch potato
a blanket of snow	is a rock	smells fishy	boiling mad

Independently Have you ever had a friend who was a lot younger than you? What was fun about your friendship? What was difficult about having a younger friend? Write a paragraph about your experience.

A. Write metaphors that could be included in a paragraph about having a younger friend. Use metaphors from the list or any metaphors of your choice.

1. _____   3. _____

2. _____   4. _____

B. Write a Super Starter opening sentence for your paragraph.

_____

C. Now make a list of events to include in the paragraph. The events should be written in the order they will happen in the paragraph.

1. _____   3. _____

2. _____   4. _____

D. Write a paragraph about having a younger friend with the information from Parts A–C. It is not necessary to include all of the metaphors from Part A. Only use the metaphors that create powerful and lasting images for the reader.

_____

_____

_____

_____

Check Your Work

Do the metaphors create a powerful image?

Whole Group Choose a sentence from your paragraph that includes a metaphor you like. Share your sentence with the class.

Add Metaphors to a Story

A metaphor is a type of figurative language that describes something by comparing it to something else. The things are compared in the sentence without using the words *as* or *like*. Writers use metaphors to create powerful and lasting images for the reader.

Independently Write a paragraph using metaphors. You may write about any of the story ideas below or think of your own.

Metaphors

has butter fingers	is a baby	heart of a lion	a couch potato
a blanket of snow	is a rock	smells fishy	boiling mad

Story Ideas

Going on a class trip   Surprising a friend
Falling in the mud   Being late for school

A. Write metaphors that could be included in the paragraph.

1. _____ 3. _____

2. _____ 4. _____

B. Write a Super Starter opening sentence.

_____

C. Now make a list of events to include in the paragraph. The events should be written in the order they will happen in the paragraph.

1. _____ 3. _____

2. _____ 4. _____

D. Write a paragraph with the information from Parts A–C. It is not necessary to include all of the metaphors from Part A. Only use the metaphors that will make a lasting impression for the reader.

_____

_____

_____

_____

Check Your Work

Will the reader be able to imagine and remember the paragraph?

Whole Group Share your paragraph with the class.

Add Personification to a Story

This page is shouting at us to begin! A page cannot shout; only a person can shout. The page is being described as if it were a person. Personification is when a writer describes an object or animal as though it has human qualities. Personification is a kind of figurative language that is used to enhance writing.

Example: *The leaves danced in the wind, acting like they had all the time in the world. The branches swayed with them, keeping time as they tapped against the fence.*

The writer uses personification in this paragraph by describing the leaves blowing and branches swaying as though they were able to dance. Personification helps the reader create a vivid mental picture of the setting and characters in an entertaining way.

Whole Group We will practice recognizing and using personification.

A. In each paragraph, there is an example of personification. First, let's underline the object or animal that is acting like a person. Then, we'll circle how the character is acting like a person.

1. **The sneakers were hiding under the bed. They were still wet from yesterday.**

2. **The car panted its way slowly up the hill, paused, then sped gleefully down the other side.**

3. **The apple was hanging on the tree, swinging back and forth as the birds sang.**

B. Now, we'll fill in the blanks with things the object or the animal could do. Use your imagination to make the sentences fun to read.

1. It was night, and one star _____ . The other stars _____ ,

   but this star still _____ .

2. The bee was _____ . He was looking _____ .

   The bee couldn't wait to _____ .

3. The ball was tired of _____ . She wanted _____

   _____ .

Independently Use personification and fill in the blanks about an alarm clock. Be creative and make the paragraph fun to read.

   The alarm clock _____ and _____ . It couldn't _____ .

   It tried to _____ , but _____ .

Whole Group Volunteer to share your paragraph about the alarm clock with the class.

Add Personification to a Story

Personification is when a writer describes an object or animal as though it has human qualities. Personification is a kind of figurative language that is used to enhance writing.

Personification Actions

dance	chuckle	sing	wink
knock	hum	guard something	

Whole Group We will write a paragraph using personification. We will describe a tree as though it has human qualities.

Brainstorming Time!

A. First, we will write ways the tree could act like a human. Use the actions from the list for ideas.

1. _____   3. _____

2. _____   4. _____

B. We will begin the paragraph with a Super Starter opening sentence. Think of some great Super Starter openings for the paragraph.

1. _____

2. _____

Vote for your favorite opening sentence.

The winning opening sentence is number _____ !

C. Next, let's make a list of events to include in the paragraph. The events should be written in the order they will appear in the story.

1. _____   3. _____

2. _____   4. _____

D. It is time to write the paragraph. We will begin with the winning Super Starter opening from Part B and include the events from Part C.

_____

_____

_____

_____

Check Your Work

Did you describe the tree with human qualities?

Add Personification to a Story

Personification is when a writer describes an object or animal as though it has human qualities. Personification is a kind of figurative language.

Anthropomorphism is making objects or animals the main characters in a story that act like people. Have you ever watched a movie or play where objects and animals were the main characters? This is anthropomorphism and is similar to personification.

> ## Anthropomorphism Actions
>
> | talk | walk on two feet | play sports |
> | eat with a fork | wear clothing | have a party |

Partners A puppet show is a type of play where puppets or marionettes are the performers. Often the characters are animals that act like people. With your partner, follow the steps to create a puppet show.

A. Think of two animals to use as characters in a puppet show. The animals will be acting like people and will be the stars of the show.

The animals in the show are _____ and _____ .

B. Write a puppet show. The show will be about the animals in Part A going fishing.

Title: _____

Setting: _____
(When and where the story takes place)

_____ : _____
(Animal 1)

_____ : _____
(Animal 2)

_____ : _____
(Animal 1)

_____ : _____
(Animal 2)

_____ : _____
(Animal 1)

_____ : _____
(Animal 2)

> ## Check Your Work
> Are the animals acting like people?

Whole Group Volunteer to read your puppet show to the class.

Add Personification to a Story

Personification is when a writer describes an object or animal as though it has human qualities. Anthropomorphism is making objects or animals the main characters in a story that act like people. Many readers think it is fun when toys or animals begin talking and having adventures.

Anthropomorphism Actions

talk	walk on two feet	play sports
eat with a fork	wear clothing	have a party

Independently Dinosaurs lived millions of years ago. Right? Then why is there one in your back yard? Write a paragraph about finding a dinosaur in your yard.

A. Have the dinosaur act like a person. What human things can the dinosaur do? Use the human actions from the list or any actions of your choice.

1. _____   3. _____

2. _____   4. _____

B. Write a Super Starter opening sentence for your paragraph.

_____

C. Now make a list of events to include in the paragraph. The events should be written in the order they will happen in the paragraph.

1. _____   3. _____

2. _____   4. _____

D. Write a paragraph about the dinosaur in your back yard. Include the information from Parts A–C in your paragraph and any other human behaviors to make the dinosaur act like a person. Use your imagination to write vivid descriptions to enhance the paragraph and make it fun to read.

_____

_____

_____

_____

Check Your Work

Do the human actions of the dinosaur make the paragraph fun to read?

Whole Group Choose a sentence from your paragraph that includes a good example of personification. Share your sentence with the class.

# Add Personification to a Story

Personification is when a writer describes an object or animal as though it has human qualities. In personification, the object or animal isn't really acting like a person; that is just how the writer is describing it.

Example: *The rose bush's vines tried to find any bare skin as I walked by, digging their thorns in viciously.*

In the example above, the rose bush isn't really trying to hurt anyone. It just seems that way. The bush can't walk or talk; it's just a bush. Personification is a form of figurative language.

Personification Actions

dance	chuckle	sing	wink
knock	hum	guard something	

Story Ideas

A kid walking through a storm   *Think: How is the storm acting?*

A person trying to get rid of a fly   *Think: How is the fly being annoying?*

An old car climbing a steep hill   *Think: Do people sometimes describe cars as though they have feelings?*

Independently Write a paragraph using personification.

A. Choose or create a story idea and write it here. Circle the object or animal that you will describe using personification.

_____

B. Write ways the object or animal seems human.

1. _____   3. _____

2. _____   4. _____

C. Write a Super Starter opening sentence for your paragraph.

_____

D. Now make a list of events to include in the paragraph.

1. _____   3. _____

2. _____   4. _____

E. On a separate piece of paper, write a paragraph using Parts A through D.

Check Your Work
Is the character's description vivid and fun?

Whole Group Volunteer to share your paragraph with the class.

Five-Story Writing Checklist

It is time for you to use all the writing strategies you have learned. You will write five different stories. If you need an idea for a story, look at the Story Ideas on page 107. You must use a different Outstanding Opener and Fantastic Finale for each story. Include as many Terrific Transitions, Awesome Adjectives, and Fabulous Figurative Language strategies as needed to make a great story. Each story will take several days to complete, ending with a finished copy for your teacher to evaluate. Use this Five-Story Writing Checklist to check off the strategies you used to complete each of your stories.

	Story 1	Story 2	Story 3	Story 4	Story 5
Title					
Super Starters					
Sound Words					
Questions					
Dialogue					
Teasers					
Setting					
Traveling Transitions					
Beginning Transitions					
Continuing Transitions					
Ending Transitions					
Clever Closings					
Memories					
Decisions					
Wishes					
Feelings					
Questions					
Electrifying Elaborations					
Physical Adjectives					
Sensory Adjectives					
Emotion Adjectives					
Personality Adjectives					
Fancy Figurative Language					
Similes					
Metaphors					
Personification					

Story Ideas

Can't think of an idea for a story? Try one of these.

You could write about...

giving a special gift to someone	a favorite vacation
having a dream	a snowy day
being president	a sick day from school
going fishing	buying the perfect gift
a play date with your friend	your worst vacation
being a hero	being an astronaut
your favorite school activity	being the principal
becoming a rock star	inventing something
creating a new game	going to camp
a family holiday	going to the beach
a day at an amusement park	finding money
a favorite TV character	learning something new
an alien encounter	performing in a play
giving advice to a friend	a huge hole appearing in your yard
your favorite book	being the star in a show
becoming famous	a talking plant
being a character in a book	winning a prize
planning a party	a hike in the woods
something you really want to do	breaking something
being in an earthquake	a mysterious sight in the sky
an argument with a friend	

_____   _____

_____   _____

_____   _____

_____   _____

_____   _____

Begin a Story with a Sound Word

Day 1, Page 6

Whole Group

1. Squeak	4. Buzz
2. Crash	5. Crack
3. Ring	6. Roar

Independently

Sound words and sentences will vary.

Day 2, Page 7

Paragraphs will vary.

Day 3, Page 8

Partners

⟨Clip-clop!⟩ As I walked into the circus tent I saw horses prancing around the ring.

"Ladies and Gentlemen," the ringmaster was shouting, "Welcome to the greatest show on earth!" Suddenly a small car came ⟨whizzing⟩ past me. ⟨Vroom!⟩ A clown was driving it and ⟨honking⟩ his big red nose. Another clown sat in a baby chair and broke it. ⟨Crash!⟩

⟨Ha, ha!⟩ I couldn't stop laughing. ⟨Growl!⟩ In the center ring, the lions ⟨roared⟩ loudly. ⟨Crack!⟩ The lion tamer's whip hit the ground and the animals jumped back on their stands. Above all the acts, the trapeze was ⟨swooshing⟩ back and forth as the performers flew from one swing to the next. It was an amazing show.

Day 4, Page 9

Paragraphs will vary.

Day 5, Page 10

Paragraphs will vary.

Begin a Story with a Question

Day 1, Page 11

Whole Group

Possible answers include:

1. What time is it?
2. Who should I take?

Independently

1. What is going on?
2. Where is it?

Day 2, Page 12

Paragraphs will vary.

Day 3, Page 13

Partners

A

1. c
2. e
3. d
4. a
5. b

B–C

Interview questions, answers, and paragraphs will vary.

Day 4, Page 14

Independently

A

Possible answers include:

1. Did / Do / Can / Could
2. What
3. Who
4. Where

Paragraphs will vary.

Day 5, Page 15

Paragraphs will vary.

Begin a Story with Dialogue

Day 1, Page 16

Dialogues will vary.

Day 2, Page 17

Paragraphs will vary.

Day 3, Page 18

Partners

A

Possible answers include:

1. Mary asked, "May I go to my friend's house?"
   "May I go to my friend's house?" asked Mary.
2. Osvaldo screamed, "I got the lead in the play!"
   "I got the lead in the play!" screamed Osvaldo.
3. The girl cried, "I hurt my knee."
   "I hurt my knee," cried the girl.
4. The teacher announced, "Your report is due on Monday."
   "Your report is due on Monday," announced the teacher.

Paragraphs will vary.

Day 4, Page 19

Dialogue and paragraphs will vary.

Day 5, Page 20

Paragraphs will vary.

Begin a Story with a Teaser

Day 1, Page 21

Whole Group

A

1. Justin couldn't believe it.
2. Gabriella opened her backpack and found money.
3. The swing was moving back and forth, but no one was on it.

B

Possible answers include:

1. Teaser (You would not sleep in a classroom.)
2. Not a teaser (It is true.)
3. Not a teaser (This doesn't seem out of the ordinary.)
4. Teaser (The sun doesn't shine at night in most places.)

Independently

Teasers will vary.

Day 2, Page 22
Paragraphs will vary.

Day 3, Page 23
Answers will vary.

Day 4, Page 24
Paragraphs will vary.

Day 5, Page 25
Paragraphs will vary.

Begin a Story with Setting

Day 1, Page 26

A

Possible answers include:
1. along
2. between
3. around
4. before

Student phrases and sentences will vary.

Day 2, Page 27
Paragraphs will vary.

Day 3, Page 28

Whole Group

A
1. beneath/under/below a bridge
2. after a rainstorm

B
Student riddles will vary.

Day 4, Page 29
Opening sentences and paragraphs will vary.

Day 5, Page 30
Paragraphs will vary.

Connect Beginning Ideas

Day 1, Page 31
Phrases will vary.

Day 2, Page 32
Paragraphs will vary.

Day 3, Page 33
1 the boy was riding his bike.
3 he went home and his mom bandaged his knee.
2 he fell off his bike and hurt his knee.

2 he was nervous that he would make a mistake.
3 the audience loved Kyle's performance.
1 Kyle practiced every day for his recital.

Phrases and paragraphs will vary.

Day 4, Page 34
Paragraphs will vary.

Day 5, Page 35
Paragraphs will vary.

Add Transitions to Continue Ideas

Day 1, Page 36
Words and phrases will vary.

Day 2, Page 37
Paragraphs will vary.

Day 3, Page 38
Possible answers include:
1. We started to pet the puppy. Soon, it wagged its tail.
   We started to pet the puppy. At first, it wagged its tail.
2. Dad said I couldn't go to the mall. An hour later, he changed his mind.
   Dad said I couldn't go to the mall. Later on, he changed his mind.
3. I got ready for the movie. After that, my mom drove me to the theater.
   I got ready for the movie. Eventually, my mom drove me to the theater.

Day 4, Page 39
Paragraphs will vary.

Day 5, Page 40
Paragraphs will vary.

Add Transitions to End a Story

Day 1, Page 41
Words and phrases will vary.

Day 2, Page 42
Paragraphs will vary.

Day 3, Page 43

How to Set a Table

Setting a table is easy when you know the proper place for everything. (First,) learn where everything should be placed on the table. When you have all the plates, forks, spoons, knives, and napkins you need for each place setting, you are ready begin.

(To start with,) put a plate on the table for each person who will be eating. (Second,) fold the napkins in half. (Then) place the napkins on the right side of the plate.

(After that,) put the knife on the napkin close to the plate with the blade facing in. (The next thing) you need to do is to get the spoon and place it to the right of the knife.

(Finally,) lay the fork on the left side of the plate. This is the last step you need to do. (Now,) you are ready to eat. Enjoy!

First	To start with	Second	Then
After that	The next thing	Finally	Now

Day 4, Page 44
Paragraphs will vary.

Day 5, Page 45
Paragraphs will vary.

Close a Story with a Memory
Day 1, Page 46
Whole Group
1. I will never forget how funny he was.
2. I had an unforgettable day with my friends.
3. Looking back, I should have remembered the time I was scared by a big kid.

Independently
Student closings will vary.

Day 2, Page 47
Paragraphs will vary.

Day 3, Page 48
Diary entries will vary.

Day 4, Page 49
Independently
A
Possible answers include:
1. memorable
2. always remember
3. brings to mind
4. remember

B–D
Paragraphs will vary.

Day 5, Page 50
Paragraphs will vary.

Close a Story with a Decision
Day 1, Page 51
Closings will vary.

Day 2, Page 52
Paragraphs will vary.

Day 3, Page 53
Solutions will vary.

Day 4, Page 54
Independently
A
Possible answers include:
1. As a result / After what happened
2. From now on / This time / Therefore
3. decided / made up my mind

B–D
Paragraphs will vary.

Day 5, Page 55
Paragraphs will vary.

Close a Story with a Wish
Day 1, Page 56
Whole Group
1. He hoped that tomorrow would be a better day.
2. Hopefully, everyone will agree, and the party will be great.
3. I wish I could have stayed longer.

Closings will vary.

Day 2, Page 57
Paragraph endings and Paragraphs will vary.

Day 3, Page 58
Student wishes will vary.

Day 4, Page 59
Independently
A
Possible answers include:
1. I am hopeful / I hope
2. look forward to
3. My desire / My dream
4. imagine

B–D
Paragraphs will vary.

Day 5, Page 60
Paragraphs will vary.

Close a Story with a Feeling
Day 1, Page 61
Whole Group
1. I am curious to find out what I will learn tomorrow.
2. She was sad but knew that next time would be different.
3. She realized that she was very impatient with her.

Independently
Feeling closings will vary.

Day 2, Page 62
Paragraphs will vary.

Day 3, Page 63
Acrostic poems will vary.

Day 4, Page 64
A
Possible answers include:
1. proud
2. upset / impatient
3. happy / delighted
4. nervous / scared

B–D
Paragraphs will vary.

Day 5, Page 65
Paragraphs will vary.

Close a Story with a Question
Day 1, Page 66
Whole Group
1. What could it be? / Where did it come from?
2. Why is she here?
3. How will he tell his parents?

Independently
Question closings will vary.

Day 2, Page 67
Paragraphs will vary.

Day 3, Page 68
Questions and answers will vary.

Day 4, Page 69

A

1. Will
2. Which
3. Are
4. What
5. How

B–D

Paragraphs will vary.

Day 5, Page 70

Paragraphs will vary.

Describe Appearances

Day 1, Page 71

A

Possible answers include:

1. young / athletic
2. powerful / graceful
3. young

B–C

Adjectives and sentences will vary.

Day 2, Page 72

Paragraphs will vary.

Day 3, Page 73

Partners

A

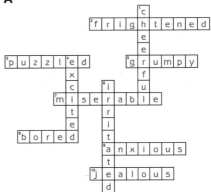

B

Adjectives will vary.

C

Paragraphs will vary.

Day 4, Page 74

Paragraphs will vary.

Day 5, Page 75

Paragraphs will vary.

Describe Details

Day 1, Page 76

A

Possible answers include:

1. spicy/delicious
2. noisy/booming
3. disgusting
4. soft/fluffy

Adjectives and sentences will vary.

Day 2, page 77

Paragraphs will vary.

Day 3, Page 78

A

It is a circus or carnival.

Riddles will vary.

Day 4, Page 79

Paragraphs will vary.

Day 5, Page 80

Paragraphs will vary.

Describe Emotions

Day 1, Page 81

A

Possible answers include:

1. frustrated
2. enthusiastic/excited
3. anxious/worried

Adjectives and sentences will vary.

Day 2, Page 82

Paragraphs will vary.

Day 3, Page 83

A

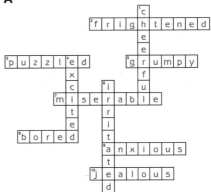

B

Paragraphs will vary.

Day 4, Page 84

Paragraphs will vary.

Day 5, Page 85

Paragraphs will vary.

Describe Character Traits

Day 1, Page 86

Whole Group

A

Possible answers include:

1. impatient
2. affectionate
3. selfish

B

1. B. wise
2. D. humorous
3. E. affectionate
4. A. stubborn
5. C. adventurous

Sentences will vary.

Day 2, Page 87

Paragraphs will vary.

Answer Key

Day 3, Page 88

A

1. conceited
2. generous
3. humorous
4. selfish
5. impatient
6. rude

B

Possible answers include:

"Give that back!" screamed Paul. Paul was very _selfish_. He never shared. He would grab things away from children and yell at them. Paul was so _rude_ that he pushed and shoved without saying, "Excuse me." Paul could never wait his turn. He was very _impatient_ with everyone. The worst part about Paul was that he thought he was the best at everything. He was _conceited_.

Julia was the opposite of her brother, Paul. Julia was always _generous_ with what she had. All Julia's friends thought she was a _clever_ girl. Julia told funny jokes and made everyone laugh. She was very _humorous_. Julia was never _lazy_. All Julia's friends thought that she was _creative_ because she could make up the best games. Being so clever, maybe Julia could teach her brother some manners.

Day 4, Page 89

Paragraphs will vary.

Day 5, Page 90

Paragraphs will vary.

Add Similes to a Story

Day 1, Page 91

Whole Group

Suggested Answers

1. like a dream
2. swam like a fish
3. as blind as a bat
4. as light as a feather

Independently

Sentences will vary.

Day 2, Page 92

Paragraphs will vary.

Day 3, Page 93

Similes and sentences will vary.

Day 4, Page 94

Paragraphs will vary.

Day 5, Page 95

Paragraphs will vary.

Add Metaphors to a Story

Day 1, Page 96

Whole Group

Possible answers include:

1. Emily _is a baby_ when she cries about silly things.
2. David _had butter fingers_ because he kept dropping things.
3. Raul thought the salesman's promises _smelled fishy_.
4. My teacher _is a rock;_ every day, he's there ready to help.

Independently

Sentences will vary.

Day 2, Page 97

Paragraphs will vary.

Day 3, Page 98

Metaphors and paragraphs will vary.

Day 4, Page 99

Paragraphs will vary.

Day 5, 100

Paragraphs will vary.

Add Personification to a Story

Day 1, Page 101

A

1. The sneakers were hiding under the bed. They were still wet from yesterday.
2. The car panted its way slowly up the hill, paused, then sped gleefully down the other side.
3. The apple was hanging on the tree, swinging back and forth as the birds sang.

B

Actions will vary.

Independently

Personification will vary.

Day 2, Page 102

Paragraphs will vary.

Day 3, Page 103

Puppet shows will vary.

Day 4, Page 104

Paragraphs will vary.

Day 5, Page 105

Paragraphs will vary.